BETH KEPHART

A PHILADELPHIA AFFAIR

TEMPLE UNIVERSITY PRESS
Philadelphia | Rome | Tokyo

TEMPLE UNIVERSITY PRESS
Philadelphia, Pennsylvania 19122
www.temple.edu/tempress

The following essays—which first appeared, in slightly different form and in some cases with different titles, in the *Philadelphia Inquirer*—are copyright © Philadelphia Media Network (Newspapers) LLC: "Preface," "Treasure Hunt," "Time In, Time Out," "The Ghosts of Bush Hill," "Them, Then; Us, Now," "Into the Woods," "River Redemption," "*psychylustro*," "City Sidewalks," "Room for a View," "The Students Stay Young; the Teacher Grows Old," "Body Language," "So Many Doors, So Many Windows," "Of Feathers and Fur," "The Artist and the Foundrymen," "All in the House," "Things Are Disappearing Here," "Essential Dualities," "Past, Present, Future," "Double Dipping," "Garden Retreat in the High Heat of Summer," "Heart on the Horses," "I Thought I Could Dance," "Accidental Tourists," "After the Storm," "Earthly Ambitions," "Notes on Her Memory," "The Lights Fantastic."

Library of Congress Cataloging-in-Publication Data

Kephart, Beth.
  Love : a Philadelphia affair / Beth Kephart.
     pages cm
  ISBN 978-1-4399-1315-4 (hardback : alk. paper) — ISBN 978-1-4399-1317-8 (e-book) 1. Philadelphia (Pa.)—Description and travel. 2. Kephart, Beth—Travel—Pennsylvania—Philadelphia. 3. Memory—Social aspects—Pennsylvania—Philadelphia. 4. Place attachment—Pennsylvania—Philadelphia. 5. Philadelphia (Pa.)—Social life and customs. 6. Philadelphia (Pa.)—Pictorial works. 7. Philadelphia Region (Pa.)—Description and travel. I. Title.
  F158.52.K47 2015
  974.8'11—dc23

                                                                2015008592

Printed in the United States of America

9 8 7 6 5 4 3 2 1

To those who have walked with me

With love

CONTENTS

III FRINGE WORK

PREFACE

Resurgent Philadelphia is cinched with light. The sun smacked up against the Drake. The eyebrow of the moon on the Schuylkill River. An argent dawn lifting lonesome hawks. Scatterings of gold.

Credit the illuminators of bridges, buildings, signs. Thank the restorers of lost or crumbled things. Consider the permutations of the new: Rafael Viñoly's Kimmel Center, Cesar Pelli's Cira Centre, Robert A. M. Stern's Comcast Center, Pei Cobb Freed's National Constitution Center, James Polshek's National Museum of American Jewish History, Norman Foster's rising Comcast Innovation and Technology Center. Walk the walk over the Schuylkill River, watch the city greenways grow, pop in to the pop-ups, make room for the cyclists, tally the famous and infamous architectural uprisings across the city campuses and health complexes. Congratulate the restaurateurs for their embrace of spill—onto sidewalks, into back gardens.

This is Philadelphia now. More than its icons, bigger than its tagline, our Quaker City has acquired something of a European glow. It has become—despite its notorious, impudent self, despite its recent sullen sulk, despite all that time when city razing was part and parcel of city planning, despite buildings that fall calamitously down, despite the ongoing struggle to serve the kids who call the city home—a place of new beginnings. The proof lies in the young careerists choosing Philly over New York, Boston, D.C. In the empty nesters, newly returned from their suburban exodus. In the eastward surge of the University of Pennsylvania and the artists of East Kensington and the hip-hop kids of West Philly and the plans made by a Pope. Recession or no recession, politics or not, notable broken things still broken, and sauciness sunk inside our DNA, something inexorable stirs.

I am interested in that stirring. I am chastened by dreamers. I advocate for hope. I see—in the restoration of rivers, in a cemetery preserve, in the interior sanctuaries of working artists, in the clang and in the quietude, in the eruptive public spaces, in the fringes Philadelphians retreat to or come from—rescue and story. For years, I've put Philadelphia inside the heart of my books—*Ghosts in the Garden, Flow: The Life and Times of Philadelphia's Schuylkill River, Dangerous Neighbors, Dr. Radway's Sarsaparilla Resolvent, One Thing Stolen.* For a while I wrote Philadelphia into the pages of magazines. Beginning in the summer of 2012, I began to catalog my wanderings for the "Currents" section of the *Philadelphia Inquirer.* I lifted my camera and snapped. By choosing to pay a new kind of attention, I saw far more than I had.

Love: A Philadelphia Affair is about the intersection of memory and place. It's about how I've seen and what I've hoped for, what "home" has come to mean to me. It's about train rides, rough stones, brave birds, rule breakers, resurrectionists, unguided and mostly solo meanderings. It is experiential, not encyclopedic. Reflective, not comprehensive. Highly personal, which is to say idiosyncratic, which is to say that my journey through Philadelphia is not over, that even now, as this book goes to press, I am walking and writing this city—remembering the hours spent with my son among the big bones at the Academy of Natural Sciences, a morning alone in the Magic Gardens, the sweet reprieve of Independence Mall during a downpour, my obsession with the town of Wayne. I'm remembering the black cat prowling near the Italian Market biscotti and the striped cats at the Philadelphia Zoo. I'm remembering the boy who sat on his grandmother's lap on the second tier at Verizon Hall in the Kimmel Center—three years old, maybe, and utterly alive as the Soweto Gospel Choir sang a reverberatory "Amazing Grace." I'm thinking of all I have yet to write whole—Passyunk Avenue, Grays Ferry, Mount Airy, the Barnes, the Navy Yard, Fort Mifflin, the food trucks, and every other corridor, institution, neighborhood, figment that you have claimed as your own.

Claim them as your own.

There is no *complete.* There is no *finished.* The city is alive, and I'm alive with it. It is old and it is new in me.

LOVE

MEANDERINGS

TREASURE HUNT

Guyer Avenue, Southwest Philadelphia

In a certain house on the 6800 block of Guyer Avenue, they rolled the rugs back to dance. They hung lucky paintings on the walls. They taped paper snowflakes to windows in winter and filled Sunday afternoons with repeated rounds of turkey, ham, and pie. In the basement they piled treasure—my grandmother's peach wedding gown, my grandfather's rolltop desk, my uncle's portraits of movie stars, my mother's report cards, boxes of gift-shop castoffs, hats inside hats, a cup of coins.

Thanksgiving lived here. Christmas. Easter. A big-eared TV in the sunroom, where Ed Sullivan conducted his business. And in the back, across the alley, beyond a fence, the ever-alive baseball diamonds and summer chlorinations of the J. Finnegan Playground.

We called it Grandmom's house. We understood, vaguely, that her terrain was Southwest Philadelphia—a row-house neighborhood set down among soggy meadows and scribbled creeks. We heard the stories about the lifelong friendships that sparked in the halls of John Bartram High, the lady faithfuls of Southwest Presbyterian, the Saturday afternoon matinees at the Lindy Theatre, the traveling photographer and his ponies, the Victory gardens that bloomed during World War II. We opened the door at the end of the narrow kitchen, slid out onto the deck, and watched the world Margaret Finley D'Imperio had chosen, the world into which our mother had been born.

It was, to us, a vast, good fortune.

I was nine when my grandmother died. She had been sick for a very long time. She called me Betty Boop and made me Easter baskets, and I knew, as children do, that I was something special in her eyes. She was my first great loss, and I feel that loss every time a holiday rolls by. My grandfather is gone now. My uncle. My mother. What remains is the house on Guyer Avenue.

A few days ago, my father drove me south on I-95, toward the airport, past the new postal center, into the old neighborhood. We stopped, first, at Southwest Presbyterian, where, on Mother's Day, in 1992, in memory of her mother and brother, my mother had had a stained-glass window installed. There are some three dozen parishioners at Southwest Presbyterian now. Many of them belong to a single family. Two of them arrived to unlock the door, to allow us in, to show us how, in a neighborhood that has endured radical change and historic tensions, they meticulously hold on.

Across the street, on a stretch of blacktop, the kids of Patterson Elementary played. In the original stone church, next to the "new" Southwest, a Head Start program was leading its charges on an I Spy hunt for color. Here, again, my father and I were invited inside. We climbed the stairs. The former sanctuary has become a staging room—an attic space filled with books and clothes, a CD player on the communion table, no pews. My father married my mother here more than fifty years ago. The peaked ceiling, he said, was the same as it had been. And so was the sun in the room.

We arrived at Guyer Avenue by way of its alley. We drove along the backs of things until we found the deck that led to the door that led to the kitchen that opened into the remembered home. It was as it always is whenever we are gone and finally return—no longer

ours. The deck was different. The door, too. The treasures in the basement—the dresses, the hats, the photographs, the gift-shop relics, all
proof of the child versions of my mother and her brother—had long
ago dispersed, blown into the wind like the fluff of dandelions.

There were no paper snowflakes on the windows.

There were no sounds of dance on the floors where the rugs
would get rolled.

The familiar aromas were gone.

I left the car, walked the alley—past the sideways shift of things,
the raking satellite dishes, the angling row-house roofline—and
entered the playground alone. The day was crisp. The sun was a
spark. My mind was all of a sudden ripe with the memory of those
summer days when I'd sit on my grandmother's deck and watch
the world beyond. Sometimes my uncle would sit there, too, telling
a movie-star story. Sometimes my brother and sister and I would
huddle close, reporting on newly found treasure. Sometimes the
kitten from next door would curl up on my lap and stay.

But sometimes it was just my grandmother and me, and I was
Betty Boop, and she was sitting close enough to share a secret, and I
was leaning close enough to hear, and this was the everything, this
was the all, this was love that lingered.

She had green eyes.

She had clouds for hair.

She believed in me.

"Do you have what you need?" my father asked, when I finally
left the playground, walked the alley, climbed back into his car.

"I always thought it was so special here," I said.

"It always was," he said.

TIME IN, TIME OUT

Riding the SEPTA Rails

I was thirteen years old when my family moved from Wilmington, Delaware, to the Main Line—thirteen when I began riding the Main Line rails. That first overheated summer I boarded at Bryn Mawr to make my way (a change of trains mid-way) to the Wissahickon Skating Club. I dressed in turtlenecks, nubby tights, skating skirts, and sweatpants—enough polyester to keep my pigtails damp as I later practiced axels and scratch spins at the rink. After that I rode the rails for the sake of city adventures or rode them as a University of Pennsylvania student or rode them home for holidays from a succession of city apartments. When work and family obligations required me to leave the city, I bought a succession of two rail-centric homes—the first set right up against the tracks (the rhythm of the trains in my sleep, the wide yellow eye announcing midnight cargo) and the second set three blocks back. I still hear the trains every morning. Their voices in the dark herald dawn.

There's something about standing on the platform watching the curve for the Silverliner. Something about feeling the rumble in the soles of one's feet. Something about the rituals of travel. Leaving and returning—that's where I've lived. I'm sympathetic to the crossties of the tracks.

Now, each spring, as an adjunct teacher of creative nonfiction at the University of Pennsylvania, I'm a Tuesday mid-day rider, boarding at Devon with my bag of books, as people have for 120 years. I choose my seat, clip my ticket, and for the next thirty-five minutes tremor toward 30th Street Station—great and white and as yet unseen. You can measure the journey in miles or by counties. You can count down the stations, every two or so miles. You can complain about all that can go wrong—enumerate your bash-ins with SEPTA travel. What interests me, however, is what happens beyond the glass—the cinema of tracks and tossed stones; the historic stations and their hats; the geography of asphalt, backyards, deserted things, and hope.

Is there anything more public than taking a commuter train? That middle-seat shuffle, those knees against knees, that girl on the videophone talking to her lover: *You know it's your turn to chase me. You know I'm waiting. You know I'll dance for you: watch.* Is there anything more private than watching the world go by through the scratched glass of a SEPTA car—the seasons unmaking themselves, the cracked trees sprouting new leaves, the fox returning to the high banks, the pink sneakers in the dirt, the stone walls black as diesel? Riding the train is riding through time. In and out. It's the slapped tail of a wild cat dangerously close to the roar.

I read the landscape according to my mood. It's either paradox or injunction, history diluted or history diverted, something clung to or something forsaken, a multi-million-dollar SEPTA surge. The landscape that lies on either side of the Main Line is a jam of discordant things, and when the light changes or a storm blows in, it's often my own face in the window that I see, the superimposition of my age against the miles.

By the time I reach 30th Street Station, I'm not who I was when I left. I de-board, descend, and walk beneath the high ceilings of the casually classical space in a meditative frame of mind. I'm aware of the fragility of things, aware of the ways we defend ourselves against change and the ways that bigger forces win. I have never once driven to my class at Penn, and I don't believe I could. Riding the rails releases the storyteller in me, breaks open the inquiry, leaves me attentive to the ultimately ungovernable collision that all teaching is.

It will be dusk before I reverse the commute—crossing the campus, ducking through Drexel, entering the side door at 30th Street. I'll walk past smoothies and popcorn to the far end of the SEPTA corridor and climb the stairs two at a time to the Paoli–Thorndale Line. I'll stand in the mirror of Cira Centre or walk east to the far edge of the platform to watch the last of the day in the city's skyline. When the R5 emerges from its underground tunnel, I'll step inside with the commuting crowd, invisible, by and large, to all the others.

The landscape in reverse will burn with the setting sun. It will clip past—the strange dystopia of the West Philadelphia rail yard, the acrobatic tags of graffiti, the profoundly indifferent Land for Sale signs, and then (all these years, and I will still be surprised) the old Overbrook station at the city's very edge. Station by station, blur by blur, the familiar and the strange will return.

I will read it all according to my mood.

THE GHOSTS OF BUSH HILL

Fairmount

Shortly after I graduated from the University of Pennsylvania, I rented the first floor of a red-brick row house near the corner of 28th and Poplar. Up three short steps, through a keyhole arch and into a surprisingly generous front room made twice its size by the largest mirror I'd ever seen. It was as if a troupe of ballerinas had lived there first. Even with my roommate gone, I was never actually alone. There were two of me alongside the ghosts of a thousand skinny arms.

I'd talked my way into a marketing job at an architecture firm in the Reading Terminal Headhouse, though my only qualification was a familial association with the man who had designed the Waldorf Astoria, the Pierre, and other mysterious landmarks. Between the apartment and the job lay Fairmount and Spring Garden. I walked the distance every working day, a jigsaw pattern running east and south just after dawn, then west and north as the sun was setting.

I was already in love with Philadelphia. This was my chance to see her anew. To imagine myself within the churn and thrum of her machine past, to find some kind of proof of the blacksmiths, iron-workers, tool workers, steam handlers, pattern makers, and sewing machine makers who had lived there once—employees of Philadelphia's vast industrial complex.

Greater and more famous than all the other enterprises was Baldwin Locomotive Works, whose smokestacks spewed and whose buildings clattered and hummed with the piece-by-piece assembly of steam locomotives and street railway cars. At the peak of its powers, according to the Baldwin historian John K. Brown, the company's shops occupied seven full city blocks west of Broad and south of Spring Garden, before finally moving to Eddystone in 1928. To walk those streets then was to squint toward them—to wonder how something so alive and thriving, so vast and reverbing, could be silenced and nearly vanquished by time.

If I walked down Hamilton between 21st and 20th and looked north toward what is today City View Condominiums, I could imagine the women of Preston Retreat, a maternity hospital for women who did not have the funds for proper care. The grand façade was gone, the catalpa trees, the garden. The rise in the hill remained.

If I walked the bridges and looked down, I could see the rusted tracks of the old railroad—overgrown by green and brambly things. If I walked by the U.S. Mint, I could imagine the refugees of yellow fever making their way to the slight elevations here, in hopes of a cure.

But no matter how I walked, I was always sure to walk down 22nd or Fairmount or Corinthian—streets that carried me past the impenetrable walls of Eastern State Penitentiary. "Grave, severe, and awful" the building is called in the pages of an otherwise cheery late-nineteenth-century guide to Philadelphia. "The effect which it produces on the imagination of every passing spectator is peculiarly impressive, solemn, and instructive." How true that was. I was young and on my own, an unforeseeable life before me. It was impossible for me to know what lay beyond the imposing edifice, what history resonated in the guard tower above, what seeds had grown to trees within the cells and labor yards, what work vandals and gravity had done since the last inmates had been driven away many years before. But it was easy to imagine the restlessness, regret, and rage that had trembled in that space. The yield of wrong choices. I would move to two more city apartments before making a life out in the suburbs. I would return to those streets in later years to visit friends. I would watch as some of what remained was painstakingly reclaimed or reimagined. As a task force of architects, historians, and preservationists would begin rescuing Eastern State from cruel proposals and long neglect, opening the building for tours and to movie directors, to Halloweeners, to artists. As a local historian named Harry Kyriakodis offered walking tours in celebration of this post-industrial swath. As an enterprising organization called VIADUCTgreene advocated for "a garden of intersecting culture and wildness along the soaring and submersive landscape infrastructures" within the former tracks of the Philadelphia and Reading Railroad. As old houses became new homes and new blooms erupted in alleyways and the conversation changed.

Appreciation is where reclamation begins. The civic enterprise of gratitude for the past that moves us forward.

THEM, THEN; US, NOW

Woodlands Cemetery

When did we become what we, on our worst days, seem to be? This nation trampled by poor compromise and misplaced screech, this drowning swell of hyper-caffeinated opinion, this landscape of the random and the ruined. We are increasingly disinclined to engage in rational debate. We rage about the inconsequential. We want to be heard, but we don't want to listen. We're quick to deplore the mess we're in and tragically ill-equipped to fix it.

Impotence has never been my thing. I believe in the students I teach, the small heroics of neighbors, quantum generosity, anonymous kindness, in doing something, making something, being something. I believe in the idea of what lies ahead, what takes us forward. We are. We can.

But when the noise of now resounds more insistently than my faith in possibilities, I head west, past the University of Pennsylvania campus, across the trolley tracks, through the gatehouses, and into the leafy atmosphere of the Woodlands. This was a six-hundred-acre estate at the height of its glory. It was home to a man, William

Hamilton, who, in the late eighteenth and early nineteenth centuries, trafficked in botany and beauty, befriended Thomas Jefferson, planted and tended the harvested seeds of Lewis and Clark, threw a picnic party on his own front lawn for seventeen thousand, and gave the United States the gingko, the Lombardy poplar, and the Norway maple. A man who would stand high on the hill, taking pleasure from the river running at his feet, the terrestrial mathematics of rocks, the gardens filibustering across the way, at Grays Ferry. Hamilton was interested in nature's boundless capacity. He reveled in it, invested in it. On the oasis of his estate, he worked to preserve it.

Today the Woodlands is a forty-five-acre National Historic Landmark, a garden cemetery in an urban place, an irregular geometry of swales and stones. I rarely see another soul when I arrive, early afternoons, some Tuesdays in spring. I silence my phone. I walk down the paths and off the paths, among Victorian funerary and planted flags, wreaths left over from another season, names I do not know, dates both recent and ancient. I teach the shaping and discovery of life stories at Penn. I teach, I hope, something about meaning. At the Woodlands, ahead of class, I walk among those who chose to embrace the ricochet of possibility and dreams, who rose above the cacophony.

You'll need a map to find the famous ones. The artists Thomas Eakins and Rembrandt Peale. The sculptor William Rush. The illustrator Jessie Wilcox Smith. The banker, philanthropist, town builder, and newspaper backer Anthony J. Drexel. The abolitionist Mary Grew. The poet-physician Silas Weir Mitchell. The Rittenhouse Square architect Wilson Eyre Jr. The Philadelphia surgeon Samuel David Gross. The honorary deputy chair of the Philadelphia Fire Department John Chalmers Da Costa, MD. The revolutionizing nurse Alice Fisher. The locomotive magnate Andrew McCalla Eastwick (who rescued John Bartram's garden from sure destruction). Paul Philippe Cret, whose architectural sensibilities infiltrated, among other things, the Benjamin Franklin Bridge, the Rodin Museum, and the Woodlands itself.

They're all here, among the politicians and Civil War heroes, the inventors and businessmen, the founders of universities and the students. Men and women who cared about the consequential, who got things done. I meander among them. I watch the birds on the trees. I make my way to the southeast promontory that still looks down on the broad belly of the Schuylkill River, though there are corroded rail lines now, and there is industrial char, there are the landscapes we have ruined and the landscapes that only the most persevering among us will finally redeem.

Who are you? I will ask my students after I have wound my way past the massive mausoleums and the humble sky-facing stones, past the gatehouses. After I have headed back over the trolley tracks and turned, my chin tucked against the wind, toward the Victorian manse where I teach.

Gridlock, gunfire, impasse, pain, and yet: Who might you be?

INTO THE WOODS

Wissahickon Creek

The day before there'd been a storm, and so the Wissahickon Creek ran freckled, like the back of a fawn. It was fifty-one degrees, the 13th of May, early, but not dawn. Fish jumped. Frogs demurred. A garden-variety Canada goose was jonesing for a show. If there were turtles on the backs of rocks, they achieved perfect incognito, and every bird that rustled was (it seemed) a chubby-bellied robin, until my eyes saw past the secrets of the trees. A chimney swift. A pair of fish crows. An operatic gray catbird wearing a sweet toupee.

There was evidence of horses. There were bikers with slender wheels and bikers with fat ones, solo joggers, ambitious dog walkers, stone-skipping teens, a man and his wife, both supported, it seemed, by a single cane. And lovers, of course. And someone posing for eternity on Valley Green Bridge. And a man who had hitched a rubber tire to a giant yellow backpack and was dragging his cargo north along the trail.

A man dragging his cargo, north.

Eighteen hundred acres of woods, and we were each on our own pilgrimage.

Like an ornate and slightly undisciplined letter J, the Wissahickon Valley Park runs long and skinny from Chestnut Hill toward Mount Airy, Germantown, and East Falls on the east, and past Andorra, Manayunk, and Roxborough on the west. Its name is said to derive from two origins—Wisamickan and Wisaucksickan, meaning, respectively, catfish creek and yellow-colored stream, and it was Lenni-Lenape territory for many years, then a Quaker paradise, then home to grist mills and other calamitous machines. Always, however, the waters ran. Always there were pilgrims.

During the planning for the Centennial Exposition, efforts were made to return the park to some of its original glory. Mills were abolished, impassable boulders removed. A walking path was set down along the west side. Visitors to the park experienced the planned revival as primeval. "The further we advance the wilder the view; every turn and bend reveals new elements and strange combinations of romantic picturesqueness," wrote the authors of *A Century After*, an 1876 publication.

Today the Wissahickon Valley Park is Piedmont territory, gorge country, famous for its schist. It's a Devil's Pool and a Shakespeare Rock, the legend of a witch, the likeness of a Lenni-Lenape, fox high on the rocks. It's haunted by the spirit of Johannes Kelpius, the German mystic who, at the end of the seventeenth century, built a tabernacle along the creek—forty rooms for forty people—and supervised botanical gardens, an astronomical observatory, a self-sustaining farm, the writing of poems and the playing of a pipe organ while waiting for the Second Coming. It fights the trespasses of manufacturers.

The park has a pair of stables, an old inn, mill shards, striped bass, tadpole communities, natural and unnatural dams, and fifty miles of up-and-down trails. It has the support and intelligence of one of the most respected organizations in the Philadelphia park system—Friends of the Wissahickon—and its history (human, geological, and otherwise) has been told in a remarkable four volumes: David Contosta and Carol Franklin's *Metropolitan Paradise: The Struggle for Nature in the City* (Philadelphia: St. Joseph's University Press, 2010). Like all urban parks, the Wissahickon has had to battle for its survival—weed out the invasive plants, shore up crumbling structures, take on polluters, redeem the trails, talk back to politicians, raise awareness, manage the deer. And while it will never be perfect, it *is*.

Sanctified and sanctifying. And every day, a pilgrimage.

There are those who forge the rocky slopes, the rooty paths, the forest ridges, the fallen trees on the back of the creek. There are those who walk slowly, then stand serene and still amid the returning birds of Houston Meadows—the black-billed cuckoo, the blue grosbeak, the yellow-breasted chat, the eastern kingbird. There are those who cast their fishing lines and those who make their way to such discrete neighborhood nooks as Carpenter's Woods in Mount Airy, where one April two years ago I discovered brown butterflies with blue-tipped wings, columns of still-deciding trees, and the legend of a school principal named Caroline Moffett who, in the second and third decades of the twentieth century, paraded children in bird costumes as part of her "mission to educate the public in the protection of bird-life," according to park literature.

But many of us, on other days, find ourselves on the wide and leafy former turnpike known as Forbidden Drive. That's where I was that chilly Monday not long ago, the gravel swishing like sand beneath my Nikes. I lost the sound of automobiles a hundred yards in. I gained the rinsed speed of the swollen creek, the operatic birds, the wind in the trees. I walked at my own pace, alone but not apart, anonymous but seen, and when this man walked by dragging his rubber sled, I turned and watched him go. He walked steadily, his chin tucked low. His power was equal to the weight that he dragged north.

We carry what we must carry into the park; we pull our own sleds. We ease into the shade of trees, stand before the ancient rocks, take solace from the rush of water that flows forward—and hope for it. There are eighteen hundred acres of sanctified land in the Wissahickon Valley and countless slabs of schist and forty-one species of breeding birds. There's what was and there's what's coming next—room enough for all of us to choose our paths and pilgrim on.

ART CENTRAL

Old City

The man I married knows the secrets of the earth. The bendable, fixable properties of clay. The elemental proportions of vessels.

I met him in Philadelphia. I waited for him in Philadelphia. He settled because of me in Philadelphia (*for* Philadelphia?), and, in time, in those two towns on opposite ends of the same SEPTA rail line. This even though he had grown up living and next hoping for a more exotic adventure—life in the jungle hills of El Salvador, a studio for the arts in Rome, a tantalizing sliver of Morocco. I have failed to intoxicate my husband with the city that I love.

"The rivers, the light, the splinted alleyways," I've said.

"But what about Seville?" he's answered.

I have meandered mostly alone and then come home to him.

But today we are together, walking the streets of Old City. A perfect, newly autumn day. The spill of coffee-shop chat onto sidewalks. An entourage of tourists massing at the headwaters of Elfreth's Alley. David Lynch's *Sick Man (with Elephantine Arm)* at the Rodger LaPelle Galleries. World War I stereographic cards and a circa-Centennial parading jacket at Briar Vintage. Cigar boxes like jewelry boxes at Harry's Smoke Shop, and vintage specs, and independent designers in art-at-their-heart shops like Sugarcube and The Geisha House, United by Blue and US*U.S. There is silence in the world's largest Quaker meeting house and a flag announcing Betsy Ross and the iconography of the Center for Art in Wood set down like hieroglyphs at the corner of Quarry and 3rd. There are spruce-smoked yellow beets and fluke carpaccios and entire Muscovy duck feasts under way at the city's best restaurant (says Kephart), Fork. The Benjamin Franklin Bridge cranks the near skyline with a sudden slice of blue.

Call it what you will: the most historic square mile in the United States. A nation's top ArtPlace. Philadelphia's most stylish neighborhood. Independence Central. Put lines around it: Front to 6th, Florist to Walnut. Understand that it is open-ended and slightly tilted, that theater will comingle with religion, that out of an industrial and mercantile past have arisen more than four dozen galleries, studios, and design centers. Imagine (or remember) not so very long ago, when you could walk this same neighborhood and look up and see naked mannequins in upstairs windows, old signs flipped on their backs, the occasional promise of a drafting table behind a padlocked door, industrial vacancy, and financial rot.

Believers made Old City new.

Believers and artists.

Today our in and out of shops and cafés is prelude. Our purpose is specific. We intercept and interrupt until we're on Cherry, just above 3rd, at the doorway to Snyderman-Works, the six-thousand-square-foot gallery with the fourteen-foot ceilings that helped catapult Old City to its current art-central standing. They arrived from South Street in the 1990s, Rick and Ruth Snyderman, bringing their national reputation with them. They built something new inside the bones of a vanquished past. They combined two separate operations into the current single whole, so that they remain one of the "oldest exhibiting galleries in the field of contemporary studio crafts" and also a very cool place to see the best of so much else.

It's the height of the ceilings, I think, as we enter in. It's the quality of light. It's the respect. No crowding of the fiberworks. Each Skeff Thomas pot on its own pedestal. The unhurried "surrender to gravity with grace" of George Mason's Hydrocal plaster, burlap, casein paint, and encaustic, *A True and Honest Friend*. Room to take it all in, to be with it for a while, to forget everything but the present now. When I turn, I see my husband in conversation with Rick Snyderman—two men talking about temperature and clay, process and accident with the intensity of those who know something more than the rest of us. Two men talking. I step away.

Art needs time, I think. Art needs room. Art requires understanding. In the old parts of a reviving city, art is a progenitor. Build it, the fashionistas, the gallery owners, the visual artists, the sign makers, and the Snydermans have said, and they will come.

They have.

He did.

RIVER REDEMPTION

Schuylkill River

Of the two rivers that carry Philadelphia's dreams to the sea, the Schuylkill has always snagged a good chunk of my heart. It feels personal to me—the Schuylkill's roving through time, her baptisms and floods, her primeval sheen, her helpless submission to toxins and sludge, her muddy regrets and redemption. The river rises and falls. She floats us on her back and steeps. She comes at us from the hills and carries on beyond us. We know her, and we need her, and she is a mystery.

When we ruin the Schuylkill, we ruin ourselves. We become, as we once were, a city with a stench, a city that festers. We forfeit all three faces of time—the past, the present, the future.

Remarkable things happen, however, when we care. When, for example, the Pennsylvania Fish and Boat Commission collaborates with the Army Corps of Engineers and the Philadelphia Water Department to ladder the Schuylkill for American shad, striped bass, tiger muskellunge, and perch—and fisherpeople return to the river's shore. When Ernesta Drinker Ballard campaigns to restore the abandoned, crusty Water Works (once a recognized jewel, once an international destination) and wins. When the Schuylkill River Development Corporation sets its mind on creating an actual riverfront destination—river access, river walks, river events, bridge enhancements, trails, a boardwalk, even—and sees the vision through.

We allowed our river to become an offensive stew, but she's hardly that anymore. We killed the fish, but they're back. We abandoned Frederick Graff's magnificent Water Works until, in 2003, it was rechristened as the Philadelphia Water Department's Fairmount Water Works Interpretive Center (FWWIC) and became the place where the story of the river and its watershed gets told. Where does the river go, and how does it feed us? Why does it matter how we treat her? Who is responsible for keeping rivers safe? What happens every time we forget?

Close to half a million people have stepped down and through the FWWIC since its opening—stood within those dampened walls, beside the old turbine and pipes, and listened to the gurgle and pulse of the Schuylkill. They have looked at river water squiggling beneath microscopes. They have counted the fish near the ladder. They have flushed the toilet and talked about the ways the river moves.

The river lives. Its rising stewards are today's microbe-counting kids. There's talk in some corners that Philadelphia is on its way to becoming America's Greenest City, a fact that likely confounds any Philadelphian capable of looking back and remembering.

But hope, like the river, streams forward. It rises and falls with each of us.

WHERE GOSSIP BEGINS

Memorial Hall

We played softball down by Memorial Hall—the Cope Linder Associates against whichever other architectural firm showed up those early evenings on the lawn. It was summer. We were young. There were rumors of a grand court beyond the granite facade, of sculpture in the basement, of an abandoned swimming pool, of police work getting done in the main hall, of minor break-ins and orchestral echoes.

We turned the rumors into gossip.

We fell in love (I fell in love) with the architect from El Salvador who showed up for softball but never played—who sat there in his painter's pants and clogs, his purple shirt, his shaggy hair and talked about coffee farms and a pair of Italian etchers and how prosperous it was to sing Cat Stevens in Roman subway stations and why it was that he'd be leaving soon for Yale. The architect who claimed that he was just passing through. The sun dipped out of sight. The shadows fell. The bats hammered the fat balls, the gloves squeezed the innings to a close, and Memorial Hall—Beaux-Arts, iron-and-glass capped, ever mysterious—stood.

The architect talked. I listened.

We returned, years on, to the place where gossip began—older now, a son between us, another book of mine in the making. I was calling this new novel *Dangerous Neighbors*. I was tying its characters and plot to the Centennial Exhibition that Philadelphia had hosted in 1876. Those nearly ten million people who had arrived at the fairgrounds just west of central Philadelphia during six months of that year. Those 250 buildings and thirty thousand exhibitors. Those exotic blooms, the ghost of George Washington, the typewriter and telephone. The lunch warmer and the stocking darner. The Pullman palace car and the Double Corliss, a vertical engine of colossal proportions that drew the close attention of Walt Whitman, who could be found sitting at its feet. The acres of new inside the Main Exhibition Hall and the miles of art inside Memorial Hall and also Shantytown, just across the street from all the Centennial commotion, where entertainment of another sort went down in taverns, alleys, and back rooms. Brick kilns and tented saloons. Salacious dens and clapboard shells. Sea cows and educated pigs, gymnasts and prostitutes, intrigue and ale, always ale.

The novel I was writing was about all that, just as it was about twin sisters of money and two young men of little means, about death and about forgiveness. In every novel I write, there is a fraction of forgiveness.

In the shadows of Memorial Hall, in the dark and leafy shadows, I walked beside my husband searching for proof of things that had happened long ago. We went up and down the Avenue of the Republic, and I imagined crowds, heat, a mash of foreign languages. We crossed Parkside Avenue and walked Viola Street, and I stopped, hoping for a rambling of gymnasts and educated animals, listening for oyster bars and the sizzling start of a fire. We returned to the gaping openness of the Centennial grounds and I tried to pace out the magnitude of the buildings long gone. We walked south again and on, searching for any speck of any part of the train depot, the

Globe Hotel, Operti's Tropical Garden, the bowls of turtle soup, forty cents apiece.

Nothing.

Silence.

Where had it all gone?

Where does it go?

We had parked at Memorial Hall, and so, when we were finished searching for things that no longer were, we returned to the only major Centennial building city planners thought to save. It had held the art of the world in 1876. It had housed the first version of the Philadelphia Museum of Art after that, also the first iteration of the University of the Arts. It had been a place to swim and a place to throw cartwheels and it had been cleaned up, finally, and carouselled and childproofed and sanctioned as the Please Touch Museum.

Sole survivor, I thought, but not really, for my husband and I were survivors, too—our three-decade love affair that began right here within the shadows. Here we were. Here we stood. I was talking. He listened.

PSYCHYLUSTRO

The Northeast Corridor

If I hadn't been looking for *psychylustro* through the dinted windows of the Chestnut Hill West train, I would not have seen the big balloon bucking at its tethers above the Philadelphia Zoo.

I wouldn't have wondered about the skinny, leafless trees (like tinder, like wishbones) or imagined nineteenth-century factory girls behind the smashed windows of abandoned manufactories or reflected on Philadelphia's history as a generative incubator of modern graffiti. I wouldn't have thought about rail-yard grass, either, or about how, despite every zooming, spewing, speeding thing, it grows.

I wouldn't have broken the rules of the Quiet Car by asking an across-the-aisle passenger whether highlighter pink is finer than seismic orange or epic green. I wouldn't have seen the horse, the solitary, sheening Black Beauty horse, flicking its tail in a garden of rubble.

Exclamatory and color righteous, unapologetic and transient, *psychylustro* is massive in scale and daring in concept, installation art that uses seven sites along a five-mile stretch of the Northeast Rail Corridor—30th Street Station to North Philadelphia—as a canvas for expression. A two-sided wall. An Amtrak communications hut. A Conrail trestle. Abandoned brick Behemoths.

They are the sorts of crumbled or ignoble structures that have, for so long, blurred by—primarily unnoticed, decidedly unhonored—as part of Philadelphia's post–Workshop of the World, post-industrial, post-tobacco-sweater-furniture-biscuit, railcar-textiles-lumber, pre-now history.

But this stretch of track is viewed by some thirty-four thousand passengers on the Chestnut Hill West, Trenton, and Amtrak lines daily. It is (let's face this fact) a portal. It required, according to Jane Golden, director of the Philadelphia Mural Arts Program, some kind of present-day attention. In the spring of 2014, the Berlin artist Katharina Grosse and a crew answered the Mural Arts Program call for an environmentally friendly (water-based and eco-tested) installation that would force passengers to look up, to see, to form an opinion.

"When we contemplate ruins, we contemplate our own future," Christopher Woodward once wrote. In the Quiet Car I ask an older man, an amateur mystery writer, to tell me his thoughts about the landscape passing by, and he tells me a story about the story he's now writing. How Philadelphia graffiti figures into it. How graffiti is a marker of time. Of the bright swatches of *psychylustro* color sprayed over brick and ballast, tree and grass, signs and glass, he says: "Looks like a professional was involved."

I ask the young conductor who rides these rails back and forth four times each day what he makes of the installation, and he cops to a preference for the midnight writings of the rogue graffiti artists who deploy not just color but also language and narrative and who work with no resources but their own, courting legal trouble. He talks about the father who took him to Philadelphia's museums each Sunday, about the art he grew up looking for, about what it means, in his opinion, to honor a place and time, about the passengers, like me, who are riding his train now looking for this art. How his train has become a museum of some kind.

Time. Art. History: that's the conversation here. The built and the fallen: that's the landscape. Also the regal defiance of empty warehouse walls and the lonesome self-supporting arches and the smokeless chimney stacks and the open-weave loom of cables and the creep of growing things over comatose things. Also the tags, hollows, bombs, heavens of graffiti angels, perhaps the ghost of Cornbread, the original Philadelphia graffiti legend. We're looking out the windows watching, and we're talking about what we're seeing, about what has been acknowledged by the electrified pink and orange and green. This isn't about color claiming a landscape, I think. It's about color proclaiming it.

And yet, this, too, shall pass. Indeed, early autumn, 2014, it is already fading, ceding to time and weather, to rain and sun blast, to the illicit tags of the uncommissioned graffiti artists. It is becoming part of the past—subsumed—so that soon it, like the black horse in the garden of rubble, will be remembered as if a dream.

What story will I tell about this pink and orange and green? The mystery writer and the conductor want to know. I say that perhaps I will write about time. Or perhaps I will write about interlopers. Or perhaps I will write about how the blast of bright things forces us to see.

Or perhaps I will write about two Philadelphia men who, like all Philadelphians, claim and proclaim for themselves.

CITY SIDEWALKS

From 30th Street Station I walk east on Market—cross one river in pursuit of another. I watch the world beneath me shift. Asphalt. Curb cut. Bridge. A ribbon of discontinuous sidewalks.

Way down deep, the planet's inner iron core radiates some five thousand degrees Celsius. Here, on the Market Street sidewalks, solidity is an illusion. The concrete panes are cracking. The bricks are buckling. The rising angles of the slate and granite tiles suggest the ceaseless motions of the earth's crust and the convective power of a restless mantle.

A planetary urging from below.

A streetscape pounding from above.

The sidewalk like geology.

Policeman boots and a transvestite's naked feet on the walk. Flip-flops, sandals, clogs, Florsheim slip-ons, tasseled loafers—the soles of the people hurrying on, taking something of the city with them, infinitesimal kernels of dust. Discarded cups and a forgotten sandwich, an arterial system of cracks, the cradled butt of a cigarette, grates, a sudden landscape of granite, bubblegum that time has turned black.

Markers of near and distant pasts.

At 15th Street, the Dilworth Plaza construction barriers are still up, so I cut south for a quick walk around, then head back through City Hall's south portal to the courtyard, where the sterile brick-and-concrete plaza embodies a faded compass rose. Here, the rose says barely, you are. In the somber heart of things. In the echo chamber of decisions made, mayoral ponderings, debate. East is that way.

And I'm headed east. I'm back on the sidewalks proper, where commerce rules, the plastic tents of discount news, the purveyors of news, the subway entrances, the downward steps to the Gallery, until the sidewalks change their tenor again, in deference to history. Keep your eyes down after 7th Street, and you'll see it—the ruddy, banded brick, the slate geometries, the profusion of tourist shoes, and then this: the inscribed names and occupations of those who lived on Market between 6th and 5th during the year of the Constitutional Convention.

Joseph Redman, Gentleman.

John Cope, Grocer.
Amos Foulke, Merchant.
Adam Boush, Reedmaker.

Simon Stedicorn, Papermaker.

Their houses aren't here, but their names are. Traces of the past on the scuffed and cracking sidewalk. Reminders of all the souls that once passed this way—the emanations of presidents and freedom builders, bankers and traders, children in their ruffled clothing, women on their way home from the open market, a cut of pork in hand, some root vegetables, perhaps a new pet bird—or a book.

The sidewalk like history.

At 3rd I take a detour and head north, where the sidewalks yield crated one-dollar records, free books in a plastic tub, fenced-in trees, grounded flower boxes, a cigar Indian decked out with a fresh-red feather, a reading man in a borrowed chair, a leashed dog temporarily left behind. There is the spill of retail and sales, the promise of something vintage, street-facing mirrors that bring down the sky. Segways. A skateboard. A hand-walked bicycle. Someone who may be preparing to sing.

On the walk along Christ Church, Mala Wright stands by her "Once Upon a Nation" storytelling bench, preparing her true stories for passersby—tales of the actress-abolitionist Fanny Kemble and the slaveholder she inadvertently married, tales of a conscientious pastor who implored George Washington to stop the terrible bloodshed of the Revolutionary War. On an average day in the summer, some sixty to ninety people will gather on this sidewalk to wait and to listen, Mala says.

The sidewalk like a credence table.

I have tarried too long. I am back on Market. I jump the final curb and follow the well-lamped curve of mostly red brick over I-95 and the Columbus Boulevard, to Philadelphia's second river. Here, at the edge of things, the sidewalk goes no farther; this pedestrian's work is done.

The sidewalk like the place a city ends.

My eyes adjust to the flow of things, to the big ships, to the brown water, to the mirage of Camden. Close in, I notice a cluster of pilings, and there, on the pilings, the single duck that has built a nest out of pristine straw. She is watching me watch her. She is brooding over the future of an egg.

Our earth is molten. Our city scuffs. There are emanating stories, one-dollar records, a fading compass rose, deep and just emerging cracks. There is new life in a river nest, just beyond our reach.

The sidewalk tells the story.

ROOM FOR A VIEW

City Hall Tower

I snagged the last ticket of the day—a tourist in my own town. Take a left and then another one, the ticket seller said. Pass the bronzed John Wanamaker. Enter the door, ride the elevator to the seventh floor, ascend with the escalator to the ninth, then wait. Someone will escort you to the top.

There were the dimensions of Philadelphia's City Hall to ponder, in the meantime—470 feet long one way and 486.5 feet long the other, more than fourteen acres of floor space, home of the mayor, the Department of Records, the Office of Public Property, the Orphans' Court, the Common Pleas Court, the Register of Wills, and that stern-faced clock with the fifteen-foot-long minute hand that has been my guide, my personal calendar master.

More than thirty years in the making, still the largest masonry office building in the states, this wild stew of concrete, stone, bricks, granite, marble, glass, and iron has gone by many names—monster, quaint, iced birthday cake—but it's standing, a fact that has never actually been preordained. It has a bunker quality down below and a radical exuberance above. It appears abundantly gray on overcast days and castle-esque when it catches the light.

When I, by now on City Hall's ninth floor, am called for my ten-minute tower tour, I am led, along with a family of three, through a pair of glass doors (keyed in, keyed out) and into the narrow cage of the tower elevator. We rise through what feels like subterranean space. The elevator door opens. Philadelphia emerges. South. West. North. East. The City of Brotherly Love.

The city seems, at first, crammed and conglomerated—a fabric of grays and blues, valves and spires, a progression of chipped heights and hardened glass, old brick, raw concrete, mechanical penthouses and golden domes, a landscape of antennae and signs. Aramark. PSFS. PNB. I have to fight the false, fleeting impression that the buildings came first and the country green later—pick-axed out of a relentlessly *built* city.

Ships on the Delaware and rowers on the Schuylkill, both rivers running bulbously out of view. The enduring nob of Memorial Hall, the tower farm of Roxborough, the hoopskirts of the convention center roof, a helicopter perched like a dragonfly on a helipad. The buildings that eventually surpassed the height of City Hall—the Liberties, Comcast—and the supreme slice of the Benjamin Franklin Parkway, LOVE Park, the burble of the Logan Circle fountains, construction cranes, the Linc, I think that's the Linc, way off in the southern distance.

The family of three is naming the landmarks. The tour giver has gone incognito. I crane my neck and look up through the clear wedges of Plexiglas to see the fifty-three-thousand-plus-pound, thirty-seven-foot-tall William Penn, with his nine-foot-wide hat and his five-foot-four feet and his mythology. He's worn a Phillies cap, this Alexander Calder statue. He's been dressed up as a Flyer. He's been buffed and cleaned and his twelve-inch-wide eyes have never so much as winked or wrinkled or flirted. Our William Penn has stalwartly seen everything.

I look back out toward the city, where indecisive clouds and reappearing sun convolute the colors, hues, tones. A passing plane brings the skyline closer. Music plays from an invisible venue. The people way down below seem suddenly nearer, caught up in their private hurry, their conversations, their transitory preoccupations on the sidewalks, the plaza, the traffic-anxious streets. They are unconcerned by the family of three and the one middle-aged woman spying down on them; they are caught up in their own patterns. They are haphazard and determined. They wear saris, running shoes, suits. They push strollers and lean against lampposts and juggle the bags of today's purchases. They, too, change the colors of the city. They guarantee that, despite all that seems fixed and crammed and stuck, Philadelphia is fluid; it's changing.

The tour guide reappears, tells us the time. Only minutes, now, to gather our final impressions, zoom our camera lenses, decide that that really is the Linc in the hazy distance, and that perhaps the music, still so pressingly near, is coming from the urban heavens. The above instead of the below. The anonymous and absolute and thrumming.

Our time is up. Our viewing done. We crowd back into the elevator with the guide who goes endlessly up and endlessly down, who doesn't, he says when pressed, have a favorite view of the sun- and cloud-stoked city. It's out there. It's porous. It lies at our feet. It takes us in. Its music falls upon us.

THE STUDENTS STAY YOUNG;
THE TEACHER GROWS OLD

Locust Walk, University of Pennsylvania

I acquire knowledge sideways and remember in shadowy bursts. University of Pennsylvania. 1978. Freshman year. Bowls of chunky granola in the dining hall. Apples the size of baby pumpkins sold from a cart. Poems in a cherry-colored box beneath my bed in a top-floor room in the Quad. The black curls on the head of a senator's son. Classrooms like movie theaters. A calculus professor so far away on his foreign stage that I wondered if a pair of binoculars might help.

(Nothing, when it came to calculus, would help.)

This was Penn to the gawky girl who dragged the aura of loneliness around her like a white cape. This, and the Russian history class she loved, and the fifth-floor stacks at Van Pelt Library, and the bookstore down beside the bridge, and, always, the soundtrack of Locust Walk, where gossip simmered, students politicked, and music flumed through the raised windows of the Greek-lettered houses that dominated the 3600 through 3800 blocks. "Let the Good Times Roll."

"Prove It All Night." "Rosalinda's Eyes." "Take Me to the River." "Don't Cry Out Loud." The music banged and slid and exulted and dared, and it was important not to take it all so personally. To let the Cars, Bruce, Billy, the Talking Heads, and Melissa just rock and roll on by. To avert one's eyes from the boys who slouched against their wide-eyed architecture.

Just two decades before I arrived, Locust Walk had been Locust Street, with automobiles and trolley tracks and the residential residue of the "suburban" district this area once was. Its conversion into the campus's main thoroughfare—its "outdoor living room"—was rapid once the cars and trolleys vanished. Steinberg-Dietrich Hall opened its doors to aspiring businesspeople. The Palladium Restaurant concocted walk-side dining. A dozen or so fraternities turned their stereos to a dominating volume. The world hurried, sideways.

Locust Walk begins in the east at 34th Street—carving a path through Blanche Levy Park, past Van Pelt and the five-thousand-pound Claes Oldenburg "Split Button," and beneath the nose of a sculpturally enthroned Ben Franklin. It cuts up past Sweeten Alumni House and Robert Indiana's tilted-O LOVE sculpture and then runs directly beneath the shade of leafy trees to 38th Street, where the Generational Bridge carries pedestrians toward an increasingly vaporous finale.

Years ago I was a student—confounded by the mysteries, dancing with strangers, embarking on a life-long thing for Bruce (Springsteen). Today I am a teacher—a spring-semester adjunct who is never lonely in the company of the heroic fifteen who sign up for my class in creative nonfiction, no binoculars required. I keep growing older—every year I do. But the young people I meet and teach are perpetually young, and they are perpetually energizing, and from them I take my hope. And though I teach in a Victorian twin on Walnut Street, I make a point to walk the Walk every teaching Tuesday. To stay attuned to all the ways it has changed, and all the ways that it has not. Call it a metaphor. Call it a way of clocking time. Call it me, Beth Kephart, trying to remember how it feels to be that young and perhaps uprooted, so that I can properly settle in and teach.

Certainly Locust Walk has been deeply diversified since my days as a heat-seeking freshman. Many of the former fraternity digs have been given over to vice provosts and graduate study centers and institutes. The former Palladium, in that grand Gothic structure at 36th Street, has become the Arts, Research and Culture House (the ARCH). The coursing brickwork has been reconfigured over brand-new pipes and electrical conduits and chilled water lines. Sometimes bright kites fly overhead, or painted squirrels sit, frozen, and always the freshmen who want to protect their good-grades mojo must avoid stepping on the inlaid rose compass at 37th Street, and now there's "Ben on the Bench" in his casual pose, at ease as he reads the *Pennsylvania Gazette.*

I walk aware of what is new. I walk grateful for what remains of the university I once knew: The green patina of College Hall. The fiery brick of the Fisher Fine Arts Library. The mansard roofs. The stone castle. The leaded windows. The ivy. And while I never hear the Cars or Melissa Manchester out on the Walk anymore (and only sometimes hear Bruce Springsteen), the a cappella artists are still clamoring for attention, and the young politicians are still advocating, and if you want to buy your tickets to the *Vagina Monologues* or the next production by Club Singapore, you can get them here.

It took me a long time to shed my lonely aura. It took becoming a teacher before I felt fully at ease with myself. Locust Walk is a river coursing, a thoroughfare, an "outdoor living room." It's where students stay young and teachers grow old, where the past is new and tested.

WRECKING BALL

South Philadelphia Sports Complex

I watch the Flyers play at the Spectrum—a first date with a first boyfriend. Battles, blood, puck, and this girl in the stands, eyes wide open.

At Veterans Stadium, I favor Steve Carlton, Bob Boone, Pete Rose, Mike Schmidt, Greg Luzinski, Garry Maddox, Tug McGraw, Dallas Green. I roar for them from high up on summer evenings, risk failing university calculus for them during World Champion season, believe in the wild mess of Phillies joy.

At the Lincoln Financial Field, May 2010, I'm part of the 55,407-person stampede at the best-attended soccer match our city's ever hosted. It's United States versus Turkey. The United States wins. We're so high up that the players look like Lego men, but I still see Landon Donovan get his two assists. I see Jozy Altidore and Clint Dempsey bang the ball into the net. I see my husband and my son, fists pumping.

I like mettle, muscles, fortitude, a long ball and a rare pass, an extra stripe of mustard on my stadium hot dogs, fireworks and LED send-offs. I'm a Philadelphia fan of Philadelphia sports teams; I own the banners and the caps. But ask me what that South Philadelphia Sports Complex means to me, and I will say "The Boss." In particular, I will say September 2, 2012, a day of rainy threats. Down the Broad Street Line I've gone. Up the steps and across the parking lot. To Citizens Bank Park, which opens like a bricky high-tech flower. Ticket acknowledged, I'm in, and now, two hours early, I meander in a nervous buzz, walking the seating bowl, taking shelter from the leaky skies beneath the cantilevered steel, trailing through Memory Lane, past those heroes on the wall, buying myself and my accompanying husband some super-sized soda from a mobile concessionaire.

This will be no lonesome day. The crowds are filtering in. Some adorned by Springsteen shirts. Some encased within hooded plastic capes. When we talk to one another, as certified members of the Springsteen clan talk to one another, we ask where the Boss, at that very instant, is. In what room, in what alley, in the back of which traveling car, crooning to whom? And has his mother come? And is Patti in the mix? And will he, looking out into the glare of adoration, see me?

The sky is the color of lead. My hair is frizz. My hungry heart has jumped its ordinary rhythms. I walk the circles, the Alley, the ramps to those breaks in the sturdy material of the park where one can stand and look out on our city. The Philadelphia skyline is a step chart. It is low rising to high then lowering back down again in intensifying shades of silver, blue, and brick. Pyramid. Spire. Slice. Antennae. Glass crescendo. Dutiful brick. The skyline on the wire.

Our seats are on the field. We head out to the temporary decking and chairs, and I hand my camera to my husband so that he can take a picture of this—me, here, at my first Springsteen concert, checking off Number One on my bucket list. Later I'll ponder the single photograph of me bejeweled by a lime-green paper wristband, the stage growing out of my head.

But right now the night belongs to us and the rain is quitting its miserly ways and they're boosting music in through the loudspeakers, juicing our joints. A friend waves from over there. The crowd packs in behind us. No hurt can be done, not in this hour, for rumor has it that the Boss is on his way.

What hasn't been written about Bruce Springsteen? He sweats through to the bottom of his boots for us. He yields the microphone to little girls in pink cowboy hats who sing the sunny day. He pounds his heart for redheads. He plays "The River" for a soldier in Afghanistan and an obscure tune for a guy with a sign. He's so present it's as if this were his first time with a crowd, though he's been traveling with his Wrecking Ball Tour for so long that we don't know how he's even standing, how he gets those guitars, one after another, strapped on, how the mike doesn't fly out of his grip, and when he bows his head beside Clarence Clemons's nephew Jake, we feel Clarence in the house. Springsteen is a stuck Catholic, a confessing romantic, a professor of truth, a scorcher and a crooner, still running, still dancing, still ad libbing, still performing. He's not out of breath, but we are, and look: he has the power to hold back the rain.

I am here.

This is what has not, until this moment, been written about Springsteen. *Kephart was here.* Having waited a long forever. Having sung him to my son. Having survived, some days, on nothing more than Springsteen's rivers—catalytic, crawling, weatherized. Having consumed countless dark hours dancing to Springsteen alone: fractured, broken, renewed, unmasked. Scoured, channeled, silted.

I have stood alone with him, and now, Good Lord, I'm here. Citizens Bank Park. The Sports Complex. The Boss as our rallying cry.

He's not done until, finally, he is. It's not over until I am back on the Broad Street Line among the clan. Until we rise near City Hall and walk the dark, wet streets toward 30th Street. My husband and I and a couple of kids just out of school, all of us talking Springsteen, all of us speaking the same language, all of us agreeing that we don't need perfection from our rock-and-roll heroes. We don't want authority. We want, most of all, to believe. To be given permission to be our own native, unrighteous Philadelphia holy selves.

IN BETWEEN

Street by Street

Six parallels named for trees: Chestnut. Walnut. Locust. Spruce. Pine. Lombard. The corners (more or less) square. Except when, to the southeast, Fitzwater, Catharine, Christian, Carpenter, and Washington twerk, and Passyunk takes off with a mind of its own. Except when, north of Arch, the Benjamin Franklin Parkway cuts a cool forty-five degrees across checkerboard squares, and Spring Garden, Fairmount, Brown, Poplar, and, for a short spell, Green raise or lower their eyebrows. Also when Ridge asserts a strictly diagonal northwest-to-southeast stance.

Philadelphia streets: They more or less behave, until they bend or break or fold or don't. I've been walking them for as long as I can remember, and when someone asks (as someone inevitably will) what part of Philadelphia I love most, I answer with the truth: I love the surprising, mutable, spontaneous things that thrive on either side of the red bricks and the marble stoops, the granite pilings and the slate roofs, the glass towers and the storefront signs, the grates and window frames.

I love what happens in between. Someone whistling. A hawk swooping. A kid up to his knees in fountain gush. A Phillies parade. Snow in the streets. The bolero I taught a friend late one night on Market Street, both of us falling off our shoes and laughing.

We don't know enough about our own lives. I can't be sure that the first time I walked the streets of Center City I was holding my mother's hand, but that is how, when I close my eyes, the past returns.

I would have been one of three impeccably dressed children. We would have been headed to John Wanamaker's Department Store with its bronzed Grand Court eagle, its Crystal Tea Room, its Christmas light extravaganza. We would have been moving through, going toward, and this is what I remember—the blur of cars on the city's streets, the red-to-green of traffic lights, the shoulder-to-shoulder of pedestrian hurry, the tail end of a fluttering scarf.

I remember the rush of things, the city alive, the alluring in between.

Later, I was an undergraduate at the University of Pennsylvania, compensating for a lonesome life by experiencing the city as theater. The buildings as backdrop. The people as players. The drama ever unfolding. Those New Market mimes. Those Rittenhouse Square buskers. That blind woman who played the spoons outside the Broad Street bank. Those fatuous stilettos of Locust Street: *Hey, Precious.* The kids chasing the smell of suds that drifted out, perceptibly, from a West Philadelphia Laundromat.

On Poplar Street, my world was movement and flicker. On the top floor of a skinny Camac Street house, I'd wait for the man I'd marry to finish two more years in another state, until the waiting felt like walls around me and I'd head off down the streets, find the trail of Philadelphia's roving roller skaters. (Does anybody else remember?) They were Super People, comic-strip heroes come to life—skating through Center City in reasonable clothes, then stripping down to suggestive somethings on a Front Street concrete plaza. They'd dance on those wheels. Toss each other to the skies. Wait for a little applause, some change in their bucket. They were nothing any architect had planned for, or any engineer had preordained, or anything William Penn had foreseen. They were speed and spin and probably just slightly illegal. They lived the in-between.

My last city home was Gaskill Street, where, now married, I'd watch the South Street party spill, the artist's car roll down the street, the neighbor lady who rustled through our trash for the fuzzy ingredients for rag rugs she'd braid. I'd watch the police trundle down our street and the holiday lights spark and the rain run from gutters, the seasons change. I'd hear the arguments the walls could not contain.

Maybe I'm not who I was, but in this way I'm still the same—seduced by the spontaneous, the protean and fluctuant and fickle. By the green apples they leave on the outdoor posts by Audrey Claire at 20th and Spruce, one of them sometimes missing. By the coleus, iresine, and potato vine of the Delancey Street window boxes—the colors perpetually mutating. By the sudden eruption of a wedding on Arch Street—the little girl forgetting her shoes. By the young woman who stands in a doorway dancing. By the unwinnable chess game at the pop-up park at the east end of Spruce. By the polar-white giant of a dog in the Schuylkill River Park Dog Run in a barking game of catch, his legs so long that some of the pups run in between them. By the young twin brothers on the Schuylkill River boardwalk who stand watching the river beneath them, the traffic on the Expressway, the gloaming coming on against the Philadelphia skyline, a turtle paddling.

The city is planned, mapped, walled in, nomenclatured. Day to day, in many ways, it is the same. What do you love most? I'm asked, and this is what I say: I love what is and then is not, what comes and goes and changes.

INTERIOR SPACES

BODY LANGUAGE

North Broad Street, Louise Reed Center for Dance

The Balanchine Trust répétiteurs are in the house—Merrill Ashley and Sandra Jennings, two once and always prima ballerinas. They have George Balanchine's work in their blood, an intimacy with the great choreographer's steps, an almost-secret knowing of how his ballets carry song.

It is noon, a warm day in October. In Studio A at the Louise Reed Center for Dance, on North Broad, Ashley and Jennings are bringing the Balanchine traditions forward—urging the Pennsylvania Ballet corps to circle their arms, extend their legs, hold very still, attend more acutely to the Tchaikovsky score.

In knitted leg warmers the dancers listen. In shear skirts and velvet leotards, in torn stockings and scuffed pointe shoes, on their toes and on the back of their heels, in the middle of the room and there, beside the barre. Jeffrey Gribler, ballet master, and Tamara Hadley, ballet mistress, are having a conversation, and now a young dancer with a question gets a quick lesson in a series of steps, and now Ashley tells Martha Koeneman, who has been the ballet's solo pianist for forty years, to begin at the scherzo again.

Sixty seconds of "Diamonds" is danced.

Ashley, wearing a blue sweater over black Lycra pants and shirt, claps and suspends the song.

Something is wrong, she says, with the diagonal.

"Diamonds" is the third act in the Balanchine ballet called *Jewels*—the final extravagance in the program that will open Pennsylvania Ballet's fiftieth season. It is a fitting selection for a ballet company that, in 1963, was formed by the Balanchine protégée Barbara Weisberger and has danced Balanchine's ranging repertoire ever since. *Jewels* is a complex ballet. It is said to have no plot. It rises from a fascination with glittering stones.

Beyond the Louise Reed Center, which fronts the quiet alley of Wood Street, the world rushes by. The impatient cars on the Vine Street Expressway. The boys of Roman Catholic High School, in their bright purple shirts. The nurses of Hahnemann Hospital getting some air, a mother hurrying her child into the Packard lobby, a student late for something at the Pennsylvania Academy of the Fine Arts, the pinkened hair and caps and tulle and shirts and motorcycle escorts of the Susan G. Komen 3-Day walkers.

But here, in this hour, the dancers of Pennsylvania Ballet are immune to all that. Their world is this studio—tall and brightly lit, a bank of mirrors in the front, Koeneman's piano to the left, a ballet master, a ballet mistress, two répétiteurs.

Into all this now step Julie Diana and Zachary Hench, the principal dancers for whom the corps quickly parts. Diana and Hench are lithe and light. They dance without pretense, gentle toward each other, leaning in to learn from the répétiteurs, who are saying something about the necessary quickness of one step, about the backward glance over a shoulder, about the velocity of spins.

Center stage and central, Diana and Hench draw lines that seem (though they cannot be) effortless. Diana is muscle and porcelain skin, black hair. Hench is charming, attentive, his hands on her hips, a word or two to a younger dancer who is confused by the placement of a foot.

Two hours later, Diana and Hench, who are married in real life and the parents of two young children, will take the floor in Studio C—alone save for Ashley, Hadley, and Koeneman. Ashley has removed her blue sweater by now. She will, over the course of this hour, dance, too—show Diana what she means when she speaks about the agitation of feet and oppositional tension, about running the circle small and then running it big but not taking it too far across the floor.

"Hit your arabesque here," Ashley will say. "Turn here. Watch him. Don't let him catch you—not yet. Yes, yes, we can see your face far longer now. Yes. This is very good."

It's the little things, Ashley says, that must be mastered now. The smallest details, the nuances. She encourages Diana to experiment with her arms, to use her back as a hinge, to take smaller steps. She sympathizes with Hench—the rapid tempo of the song, the athleticism required at the end of a sequence for which even this large room is too small. Diana and Hench are intelligent dancers—unafraid to ask, quick to assimilate, capable of laughing at themselves. Ashley is empathetic, generous, transparently wise. Theatrics and technique are her stories.

It is exhausting, Ashley tells Diana and Hench. It is beautiful, she assures them. It must be a little more like this. A black curl has escaped from Diana's bun and spirals partway down her pale forehead. Out of breath, in her fourth hour of rehearsal now, she works the sequence again.

There is the sun falling through the clerestory. There is the sound of a piano in an adjoining rehearsal room. There are the repetitions this répétiteur requires, the heat in Diana's face, the rasping breaths at the end of each sequence. The hard work is hardly done, and now Hench begins a succession of leaps around the room—his body upright, his hands full of grace, his legs scissoring open, scissoring closed. When he is done, he stands by the barre, clasping his hands to his knees, breathing hard. It is Diana's turn now for a solo run, and she summons all her beauty and turns.

At the barre, Hench looks up and watches his wife spin and blur. The charm in him becomes the way he looks at her—a lucky man in their world.

SO MANY DOORS,
SO MANY WINDOWS

Wayne Art Center

Once, when I was eight or maybe nine, I drew a butterfly. Its wings were symmetrical, more or less. Its colors were just this side of natural. Its antennae bore a clever curve. On that day I was an artist.

Artist. What rapturous possibilities, what secret skills and power. In all my years post-butterfly I've never again attained such glory. My middle-school dioramas were sturdily glued. My poster of deep-sea creatures had a few nice hues. My beaded jewelry was primarily obsessive. I couldn't draw a thing.

Over a long stretch of my long life, I've circled that kind of art, lived it in the proximate. Gone to the museums, navigated the fringe, worked for the architects, novelized artists, married that man who kept linseed oil in the pantry by the fridge. Art (that kind of art) was something I observed. And then my husband bought us time at the Wayne Art Center.

I thought he was kidding.

He swore he was not.

For the past year, then, once most weeks, I've been taking lessons in clay, which is to say pinched pots, fab slabs, slumped humps, slipped scores, darting and seaming. I stand among persons of talent (that artist husband included) with my poundage of stoneware and try. I dig, from my tote, the knives, the loops, the rasp, the kidneys, the pretty little pots of underglaze. I slice. I roll. I cut. I smash. I wedge the clay, start over.

The math of making pots frankly escapes me. The mysteries of slip and wax resist are deep and many. The language of muck is viscous. There are plenty of ways to ruin clay.

I ruin. I persevere.

Nested between a nature trail and the heart of Main Line Wayne, eighty-five years old and ever inventive, the Wayne Art Center has the hint of the palatial about it. It has many doors and many windows, rooms for making and rooms for seeing, a super-sized kitchen and a lobby so capacious that people can sit at tall tables, head for the gift shop, or haul in their easels, glassware, or yarn and never feel crowded or pressed. The making of art is the journey we take. The center specializes in journeys. Through a series of considered expansions, it has maintained the fervor of its original founder, Quita Brodhead, who began offering art instruction to children in a carriage-house garage on Louella Avenue in 1930.

The center, which caters to some five thousand kid-, teen-, and adult-aged students as well as an estimated twenty-thousand visitors each year, provides instruction in fine arts, crafts, the art of the kitchen, music, and drama. It offers juried exhibitions and gallery shows, team-building exercises and lectures, programs for the underserved. Still lives, clay frogs, book art, stained glass, plein air, international flavors, wax casts, bangles, glass forms, raku, a little theater: this is the center, too.

In the pottery studio, where I spend three hours each week, the center also yields a rare form of community. People with skills advising people (that would be only me) without them. Encouragement hummed, sometimes even sung. Celebrations of the immortal kind.

Homemade cookies, salads, breads, dandelion wine. An extraordinary quantity of laughter. Lessons in what we like to call "our social skills."

Have some.

Try this.

See what you think.

You're kidding.

Over the spinning of wheels, the rasping of clay, the stirring of glazes with toilet-bowl brushes, there is talk. Of books, of cinema, of Brooklyn. Of Gordon Lightfoot and Berlin. Of advertising careers and *Star Wars* heroes. Of recipes and garden seeds and bagpipes. Pots are getting built, tiles are being tested, faces are being carved into greenware towers. Someone offers up fistfuls of hand-colored clay. Another extols the wonders of Shino. Someone suggests that more is more, and that the accidental must be honored, and then E. will walk in with a new pair of painted sneakers, and the talk will turn to her impeccable style.

A gathering of fans around E.'s impeccable style.

There (and not on the periphery) I stand. Wedging, rounding, mounding, slicing, mitering, giving the clay room to do its thing. I am laughing. I am listening. Because the thing I've learned best throughout these seasons of clay is that I don't have to be excellently good at this to enjoy it. I can start at 9:30 and leave at 12:30 and not have accomplished a darned clay thing, and yet the hours will have value—tangible if not precisely quantifiable. I will leave the center feeling a little more free, a little less dutiful and proper.

I will know myself to be the outsider who has found her way in. So many doors. So many windows.

OF FEATHERS AND FUR

The Martha Street Hatchatory, East Kensington

They are in the wind and in the faces of the rivers. On the rooftops and in tree nooks, in the green of the squares, on the lips of the fountains, on the library steps, on the rim of William Penn's hat. They were here before the city was, before the Lenni-Lenape, even, and they (the peregrines and hawks, the finches, pigeons, chickadees) are, today, our urban warriors—on guard, in transit, adaptive, dialing up the volume on their songs. They fly according to no grid. They sing when they want to.

In her early twenties, Beth Beverly—a young jewelry maker— found herself obsessed with the beauty and plight of Philadelphia's birds. She was dressing windows for Daffy's at the time. She would hear the thump of a bird against a window, and it would, she says, "crush" her. "There was this beautiful creature," she explains, "suddenly still on the sidewalk, beneath the feet of crowds, being pushed toward a gutter." They were birds in need of some kind of rescue, and she made herself responsible.

Their feathers intrigued her—plumes and down and bristles. The shape of their claws. Their bony beaks. This jewelry maker who had, even as a little girl, glued yarn to barrettes and pierced shells to make earrings began to use the parts of the birds she'd found as "adornments." Flight feathers in a hat. Claws in a necklace. Bones in dream catchers. The tip of a tail feather in a necklace. She discovered an old text on taxidermy in a used-book store and taught herself the rudiments of the trade. She learned about life by studying death, and when she could not teach herself more, she headed off to the hills and spent three months gaining knowledge, and a certificate, from the Pocono Institute of Taxidermy.

Reality-TV producers and documentary filmmakers—AMC's *Immortalized* and *American Hipster*—noticed this impossibly gorgeous woman with the perfect profile who made things out of fur and feathers (and, increasingly, preserved pets); they featured her prominently. Clients arrived and multiplied. A private passion became a life's endeavor. Beverly's hats and fascinators, hair sticks, brooches, and earrings acquired a following.

Today Beverly is one of the two dozen or so artists at work in the Martha Street Hatchatory—a late-nineteenth-century brick building in East Kensington once famous for the manufacture of soap. The Hatchatory is integral to the artist revolution that has swept through this corridor over the last several years—a proud building with wood-planked floors, a funky working elevator, and surprising views.

Beverly herself looks out toward the Delaware and backyard gardens, toward the trees that rustle every time the El whooshes, toward a faraway building with intricate spires that she has claimed as her personal castle. She works surrounded by the things she's made, the birds she's known, the animals that have come to her through (she again emphasizes) ethical means—natural and accidental deaths, creatures grown by farmers as food.

Down the hall is a recording studio. Nearby, a professional makeup artist. And, outside, Frankford Avenue runs at its renegade angle, breaking the stalwart Philadelphia grid to make room for those working on the fringe. Unnecessary rules don't break the artist spirit on the Frankford Avenue Arts Corridor, Beverly says. The New Kensington Community Development Corp., the early promoter of the corridor, remains committed to the artists—making room for First Friday arts gatherings and local galleries and workshops. People who need space and time and affordable rent are, in other words, welcome here.

Beverly's work, she'd be the first to agree, is hardly ordinary, especially in an era in which Americans are often uncomfortable contemplating death, witnessing it, wondering about the aftermath. We eat our food, but do we always consider its origins? We hear a bird thump against window glass and we hope, sometimes against hope, that it will simply fly away.

But Beverly sees, within the stilled furred and feathered things, a "radiating positivity." She sees a place for sparkle. She sees, most of all, the miracle that life is and the majesty of nature. She points to a pheasant that sits stuffed in a box by my elbow and begins to name its countless colors. She tells me the goat that wears the pinkish crown is her friend Harriet, who died in childbirth. She says the bear whose glittering paw holds her business cards was a gift from another taxidermist. She says that some don't understand her twinned fascination with beauty and morbidity, but she can't imagine doing any other thing. In a beautifully restored brick building, in a part of town that welcomes artists, she is among the things she loves.

A perfect artist's life is a just-enough life, Beverly says—a Goldilocks life. Enough recognition to be respected by those she meets. Enough money to live comfortably with her artist-musician husband. Enough clients to keep doing the work that she loves. Maybe, someday, she'll have a handful of high-end clients—a Lady Gaga—whose investment in her work will allow her to create some of the fantasies she has in mind. Maybe there will be more who turn to her for the forty or so pieces she builds each year.

For now, Beverly has a possum tail to weave into a silver chain. She has the breeze. She has her views. She has feathers on her desk, fractions of wings.

WHERE LITERATURE LIVES

Free Library of Philadelphia, Central Branch

It is a rare day in winter—dry, blue skies and thin, sheeted clouds. On the streets of Philadelphia, people are taking their time—pausing on the bridge above the swollen Schuylkill River, eating frozen yogurt on a bench in Logan Circle, encouraging a carnival of birds near the base of the Shakespeare sculpture. Outside the central branch of the Free Library of Philadelphia, three men are arguing the way that friends do—not to win but to exercise ideas. They keep a vague watch over the library doors, where, like so many T. S. Eliot characters, the women (and men) come and go.

The great lobby of this palatial Beaux-Arts structure lies just beyond those doors—vast, polished, and presided over by a couple of guards and a bronze statue of William Pepper, the physician and former University of Pennsylvania provost whose conviction (and uncle's money) spurred the creation of the free library system that now includes fifty-four city branches.

It is said that some seven million items can be found here at the central branch. Books and maps, medieval manuscripts and holiday postcards, choral music, stereoviews, automobile wiring diagrams, aerial photos, albumen portraits, rare books, film stills, early children's literature, photographs of horse cars, Dickens memorabilia, old novels, new novels, a stuffed raven. If you want to read a book, if you want to write one, if you are searching for a job or hope to concretize a calling, if you are impassioned, if you are bored, if you aren't sure and especially if you are: come. Everything is here.

In my own travels among seven million things, I've happened across centennial-era tickets, nineteenth-century hotel brochures, menus featuring turtle soup, first-edition journals, dusty newspapers, rare prints of my river, first-person accounts of the wonders of a lost world, a photograph of a Zeppelin casting its shadow over the city, antique women's journals. The factual and the artifactual. The absolute and the imagined. Persuasions, possessions, borrowed words, thoughts that crowd the margins. A library is the story of us. It is time kiting backward and forward. Within the marble and limestone of the venerable central branch, something is always astir.

Today, for example. Today, in the Montgomery Auditorium on the building's ground floor, work is under way in advance of one of the nearly 120 author events hosted by the library each year. Tonight's sold-out affair features the political warriors and lovers James Carville and Mary Matalin. A banner is getting hung, books are being delivered, consultations are occurring in code, and soon extra chairs for the overflow will occupy the library's grand lobby above. Something big is happening, again, in Dr. Pepper's library.

Down here, behind the auditorium curtain, the green room is bright with lit bulbs, repeated mirrors, and the shiny faces of the signed posters of the authors who have been here before. Chimamanda Ngozi Adichie. Jimmy Carter. Junot Diaz. Maureen Dowd. Julius Erving. Tina Fey. Jennifer Egan. Anchee Min. Isabel Wilkerson. Jill Lepore. Pete Townshend. Amy Tan. James McBride. A. Scott Berg. Elizabeth Gilbert. Chip Kidd. Samantha Bee. Doris Kearns Goodwin. Jeremy Scahill. Erik Prince.

It is a rotating cast of characters—the big, beating heart of literary culture in Philadelphia. It is the place where anyone can come to be entertained, to be ascertained, to be provoked, and if James Carville and Mary Matalin are not your cup of tea, just wait. In the days to come, E. L. Doctorow will be here. So will Jane Pauley, Gary Shteyngart, Kevin Powers, Wendy Lesser, Ishmael Beah, Ransom Riggs, Sue Monk Kidd, Nancy Horan, and, later, a pair of Nigerian writers whom Andrew Kahan, the Ruth W. and A. Morris Williams director of author events, is eager to showcase.

The point is it never ends. Kahan makes sure that it doesn't. Articulate, discerning, charming, and a master of the memorable e-mail, Kahan makes it his business to draw the most interesting writers working today to Philadelphia, a city that would otherwise be overlooked on many author tours.

Kahan wants, he says, his audiences to sit in the auditorium or the overflow chairs and feel some version of wow. He wants Philadelphians to participate in a national conversation, to stand beside a movie star, to shake the hand of a politician, to ask a novelist how fiction gets done. Controversy does not concern him. Keeping "what passes for the soul" engaged does. And so Kahan reviews the innumerable books and press releases that come to him each year and makes the call, then hosts his guests with care, leading them back to this brightly lit realm, this pause before the show.

Seven million things at Dr. Pepper's library, I think, standing here beside Kahan in the green room. Seven million things and also, 120 times each year, the evanescent art of authorial conversation. Libraries put the possible within reach. The ideas: they come and go.

THE ARTIST AND
THE FOUNDRYMEN

Port Richmond

I take the Blue Route south and I-95 north. The day is gray and bitter, the lanes too aggressively pocked. Beyond me the Delaware River crawls, heavy with the exhaust of bedlam truckers and implacable with its reminiscence of pirates, oil tankers, and whale bones.

At the Allegheny/Castor Avenue exit I veer right then left toward the heart of Port Richmond. This was collier country once—home to coal traders but also shipbuilders, cargo holders, and dockhands. The houses are trim. The streets are clean. The bakeries promise Polish sweets, the churches Lithuanian hymns. I park on Allen Street, beneath the rumble of the interstate overhead and alongside the blank stare of former tall-necked warehouses.

The door to Jeb Stuart Wood's Independent Foundry is here on Allen Street, sitting high in its frame, unmarked and unlocked. I step up and into a fantastical world of green filtered light and barrel drums, ceramic cavities and kilns, bronze busts, a primal table, a metal-armed octopus, the roots and hollow of a cast tree stump.

Bicycles are strung from wooden beams. Wax slops around in a pot. An orange cylinder blows heat into the chill. There is an exhumation of dust.

Now Wood himself appears from a room in the faraway back. He has degrees in fine arts and biochemistry, a flannel shirt, a thick plume of hair beneath a modest cap, and he's a foundryman, an artist. Some of the most important artists of our time entrust Wood and his colleagues with their casts. One of them—Michele Oka Doner—is on her way for a visit from her famous loft in New York City (think Patrick Swayze, Demi Moore, and the movie *Ghosts*, and you have seen her loft's facsimile) to check in with a new slate of work.

Michele Oka Doner. If I were reading this aloud I would pause while you Googled her work, her acclaim, her style. I would let you stroll at leisure through her resumé—a word that feels just a tad impoverished when you consider all that she has done. If you've visited the Metropolitan Museum of Art, the Art Institute of Chicago, the Musée des Arts Décoratifs at the Louvre, and the world's great galleries (among other places), you've seen her tattooed dolls and death masks, figurative sculptures, furnishings, jewelry. If you've traveled through the Miami Airport, the Ronald Reagan International Airport, the Herald Square subway station in New York City, the Hayden Planetarium, a flagship Tiffany store, the largest luxury mall in Qatar, three U.S. courthouses, or Philadelphia's own Criminal Justice Center, you've been touched by her art; it has touched you.

Oka Doner believes in beauty; she was brought up in beauty's faith. Her father an intellectual and a lawyer and, for several years, the mayor of Miami Beach. Her mother a Latin teacher fluent in many languages, a minimalist, a proponent of good taste. Oka Doner's childhood was rich with the gifts of the sea, the sound of palm-tree rustle, the seizing spark of violent weather, the glamour of seeds and busted pods. She was given the freedom to explore the natural world and the provocation of dinnertime conversation about books, justice, art. From all of that, she emerged as a woman curious and grateful, as a poet-artist who sees herself as a vessel, cites poetry from memory, and named her first son for a river.

When the sculptor arrives in Port Richmond on this cold, gray day and enters the foundry, she is bearing gifts. A box of cookies for Wood and his artist-foundry cohorts. Two books for me. She looks at once for her pieces in progress and settles in with the radiant disk table, the fourth in this series, which awaits its final touches and will, when complete, gleam in her loft home. Ferric will be applied—a light patina. During the ensuing conversation about application methods, Oka Doner listens to what the foundrymen say. She dons a face mask. She focuses on flame and craft and form. "Beautiful!" she says, over the hiss and sometimes silence. "Beautiful. You've done a wonderful job. Not too orange. Just gold, and right."

In time her attention moves to the stump of a tree that has been cast for a private client in the South. It, too, must be patinated, finished, but now as Oka Doner discusses the possibilities with the foundry artists—liver and ferric? only ferric?—she asks for a brush, pulls on a pair of mismatched gloves, and applies the patina herself, eager to get to the crannies and textures, pleased with what this sculpture has become, what it will be. The stump smokes with the applied heat and chemicals, volcanic. She leans toward it—limber, funny, enthralled, grateful for the care of the Port Richmond artists who have given her work-in-progress a sheltering home.

What does it take to run a foundry in Port Richmond at a time like this? Love for process, Wood says. Love for handwork. An understanding of the steady momentum gained from positives recalibrated into negatives recalibrated into positives again. It's a little like Port Richmond itself, a place Wood describes as gratifyingly tight—a little dirt beneath its nails, a lot of pride about its past.

ALL IN THE HOUSE

Reading Terminal Market at Thanksgiving

It is the mustard at Salumeria that makes the sandwich. It is the powdered sugar that completes the plumped-out Beiler's doughnuts dough. It is the fact that the chocolate is still a molten mess inside the Famous 4th Street fare that renders those cookies so irresistibly fine. It is the sweet in the savory of Original Turkey specials that you remember later, that you speak about, to friends.

"The long line of stalls stretching away and diminishing, hung with all manner of farm-yard and forest marketry; the crowds coming and going in the main avenue; the receding rows of lights overhead; the color, the movement, the life—who can describe it? Dazzling and bewildering as a whole, it is enjoyable only when studied in its details. . . . You can find everything here in its season, and better than you can find it anywhere else."

Those words were published in 1876, in Edward Strahan's *A Century After,* about a "Farmer's Market at Twelfth and Market streets." The writer may have been speaking of "calves, sheep, and swine," "potatoes, corn, wheat," "peaches, plums, pears," and "partridges, woodcock, snipe, reed-birds, rail, and canvas-back ducks." But he was speaking, mostly, of the experience. The pleasant yammering of the crowds. The craning of the necks. The anticipation.

Try some.

Earth. Griddle. Fryer. Canisters. Cartons. Buckets of ice. The back edge of a knife. Silver skewers and plastic shovels. The invitation of open hands. Reading Terminal Market fare at 12th between Filbert and Arch all comes from somewhere.

And so do the crowds.

It is almost Thanksgiving. Outside the air has that leaves-have-fallen bite, the convention crowd is surging, the traffic is in budge mode. Inside, coats are hooked over the crooks of arms, the fingers of the piano player insouciantly glide, the flour rises to cumulus heights in the sky above the Flying Monkey, shellfish shiver, and there's a bright, mad game of musical chairs going down among the lunchtime crowd.

This abundant, bristling market is, in November, the most un-lonesome place around.

All these turkeys taken from the farms (and plucked). All that pumpkin in the pies. All the eggs in their cartons and the preserves in their rows and the coins slipped between the lips of Philbert the pig. Everyone feeling more generous now, defying the coming dark of winter and the drone of bad news with clustered flowers and extra ketchup and some pre-turkey chowder.

The crowd is jammed into Molly Malloy's. It is shoulder-to-shoulder by the Termini Brothers biscotti. It is taking shelter in the Down Home Diner, appraising the ducks at Sang Kee, angling for stool space at Profi's Creperie, calculating the expression on the well-shod figurehead who gleams from her perch above Pearl's Oyster Bar. Is she angry? Is she love-struck? Is she sad?

The crowd *is,* and maybe we are what we eat, but I'm of the opinion that we are also the tall bar stool, the burgeoning paper bag, the sticky chocolate fingers, not just the piano but also its tip jar, the figurehead, the sheltering roof. I am persuaded that we go to the market not just to buy but to be part of the crowd, to fit ourselves inside it, to confirm that here, at least, we are part of something, we are in this together, this season soon to come.

We stand in lines exchanging recipes. We offer tips on thawing time. We establish stuffing preferences, reveal the secrets of our soups, point to a stall across the way where they have (we're sure) just what this man beside us, that woman down the way needs. Our bags are fat with poultry, cranberries, squash, bouquets of mint and basil, cake. Our bags are: What we have chosen. What we plan to carry home. What we believe about the gifts we're capable of. Our bags represent the care we mean to take of the people we love, the family and friends who will be coming soon.

At the Reading Terminal Market, against the backdrop texture, taste, and smell, our season begins. To strangers we tell stories about the idiosyncratic dish, the flecked black pepper, the cakes our mothers made. To people we'll likely never see again, we say, *I'm hoping for*. . . . And then we go on, unhook our coats from the crooks of our arms, and head back out into the nipped air and toward our homes, where the color, the movement, the life will continue to unfold.

THINGS ARE DISAPPEARING HERE

Fairmount Water Works

It is the title of a Kate Northrop poem. It feels, at times, to be the state of our existence. It is the sentence I read to thirteen rising eighth and ninth graders on a thickly humid day in the belly of the Fairmount Park Water Works.

Beyond me, the Schuylkill River runs high and muddy in the wake of last night's storm. Down the halls, children are learning the history of water, how it moves, what it needs, why it matters. Here, before me, sit an amateur ornithologist, a rapping quarterback, a girl who admits to four-language fluency, a boy known for loving the color green, a girl who smiles dreamily when she thinks about her hero.

"Things are disappearing here," I say again, and now we together build a list of the things we are in danger of losing, the things we must protect: Asian elephants, Bengal tigers, love among humans, an ability to control our own greed, the chance to return to the day we are right now living, the California condor and the Philippine eagle, and also peace, friendship, freedom, wisdom, imagination, time.

The disappearing list is a warm-up exercise for my day with the children of Project FLOW, a five-week, daily intensive summer program designed to allow a small group of curious students to explore water as artists, historians, scientists, and social activists. Ellen Schultz and Chris Singler oversee the program, and this summer two teachers, Rachel Odoroff and Joy Caldwell, lead it. The program is one of the many reasons the Water Works has been named the Delaware River Basin's Official Watershed Education and Gateway Center for the Schuylkill River National and State Heritage Area by the Pennsylvania Department of Environmental Protection.

So far, these kids have toured the river, learned the power of watersheds, walked along the Wissahickon Creek, shared a boat ride with young people from a Texas town now living with stage-three drought. I'm here to talk about the river's soul, her voice, her destiny. I'm here to listen, and it is clear to me within a mere ten minutes that these gorgeous, funny, audacious kids could go on and on, fill several sheets with lists of disappearing things. It's clear, too, how much they care, how much attention they are paying to the world, how unhappy they are about the mess they've been left, how determined they are to make a difference. There's more, there's more, there's more, but we move on. We must. The morning grows old.

I ask the children to consider the emotions of the Schuylkill during the recent storm. Empowered, alive, worried, trusting of the moon, I'm told, and then Raymond Rochester-Pitts, the budding ornithologist, adds that the river, while feeling big and powerful, also felt sad about all that pollution and debris.

How, then, I ask, did this river, with all her feelings, all her capacity, come to be? Write me her creation myth, I say, and Sashoya Dougan writes of a humble girl hoping to be important, a single drop that finds its way to the mortal world:

I was finally important, but after years and years people got lazy and harmful, they would throw things at me and ignore me. I longed to be home again, but this was my life now and I had a duty to uphold. I watched as the world around

*me turned the beautiful green land into rubble, gravel, and
smoke. Not only was it killing the animals that I called friends
but it was clouding the spirits of humans and their offspring
and it continues to. I am now an old woman. I've seen things I
cannot explain, but I've also seen a small but great amount of
humans who will want to and have helped this world become
healthier and greener. I don't know how much longer I will
flow, but I pray to the gods that created me that I will live to
see the day that our world is green again.*

We're only just getting started, and look. We've only just begun
to talk about voice and nouns, verbs and monologues, the river's
heart, her love affair, her needs. Every child here has something to
say. I ask them, now, to imagine themselves taking a walk beside our
mayor on the river's banks. What do they ask him? Ellie Cheung:

*"When do we know that the river has been fully restored to its
    original beauty?" I said.
"I can't say we ever will. But we can do the best we can," he
    said.
"How does one know that it's good enough?" I said.
"When we are satisfied," he said.
"But what about the river? When will it be satisfied?" I said.
"I don't have the answers for the river. I only have the answers
    for us," he said.
"Then who has the answers for the river?" I said.
"I don't know," he said, sighing.*

"'Love' is a strong word, something that cannot be explained,"
one of the students says, a few moments later, as we work on a poem
about those things the river loves. Yes, I think. Love cannot be
explained. But how I felt it in that room.

ESSENTIAL DUALITIES

Philadelphia Museum of Art

I had been too long gone. On this day, I was home. Tomorrow the winds would howl, but today was sky blue calm. Tomorrow the world would rush and I would worry. Not now.

Right now was the man I love, beside me, the goofy foots and grinds at Paine's Park, the river otter out for a swim in the Schuylkill. Right now was the Spring Garden Bridge wrapped like a Christo sculpture and the tall fringe of November weeds along the banks and the miles of no cars and the tens of thousands of runners—marathoners, half marathoners—who had come from all around the world to run forward into history.

Some of the runners had already crossed the finish line and were among the walkers now, wearing their silver Super People capes and medals. Some were holding their own signs as they trotted, shuffled, moaned past the mounted policeman and the Perelman Building and the waiting-for-Thanksgiving stands, as they made their to the Benjamin Franklin Parkway finish, where an emcee with a broadcast mike was calling out the names of the winners. Winner. Winner.

Winner. Everyone a winner. So many winners that even those who
had not run triumphed according to proximity.

You could hear the ricochet of names up along the stone wall of
Girard College. You could hear it on Ringgold Street and down by
Eastern State Penitentiary and inside the London Grill on Fairmount
Avenue, where the ghost of Willie Sutton is said to live and where
they were tuning their TVs in preparation for the Eagles' tromping
of the Titans. You could hear it in the shadows of the Fairmount
Park gazebo and by the Franz West *Lips* in the Anne d'Harnoncourt
Memorial Sculpture Garden, but you could not hear it inside the
dolomite vault of the Philadelphia Museum of Art.

It was nearly silent there.

It was almost still.

The day had only newly begun in the Dorrance Galleries, where
the work of the photographer Paul Strand hung. Gray tones and
birch trees and a stolen yawn. A mother in a doorway with her
sons. The scroll of the fern, a child's stare, the famous long shadows
of *Wall Street*. Glass plates, cameras, travel logs. The first wife. The
last one.

We had slipped inside, my husband and I. Left the boomerang
of the marathon, and we were walking, room by room, turning the
corners, stopping to see. We were holding hands, or standing far
apart, while outside the runners ran, and their fans cheered, and up
and down the parkway and in the red-brick alleys and maybe even as
far as Manayunk the names of the winners were called.

I studied the deep sepia smears of the frozen moments. I followed the gaze of the portrait subjects whose worlds had slipped
on by them. I wondered about the girl who carried the books on
her head, and had she read them, and how had Strand persuaded
her to stand against that wall and cast her eyes so unselfconsciously
down, and what had she become? I thought of all the times that this
museum had left me steeped in some version of awe. How it had
hushed me when my child was young and taught me as I learned to
teach. (What is color? What is landscape? What is story?) I imagined
the memoir I might write around the paintings, the teahouse, the

armor, the hats, the borrowed collections and the permanent ones that infiltrate a life and a way of thinking. I thought of how this museum sits high on a hill and how it had once been (the metaphor so rich) the city's reservoir.

Outside, in the streets, the winners ran, the crowds surged, the silver Super People capes caught the sun. Here, in the Dorrance Galleries, the photos of people and places now mostly gone hung quietly. A city is snap and still and art on the hill, a man and his wife and a victory crowd. A city is dualities, complexities unwound. We win by proximity.

PAST, PRESENT, FUTURE

30th Street Station

On sunny days, the boxed-in air of 30th Street Station is bronzed and the trapped birds fly at rushing angles toward the vertical glass. When it rains, when it snows, when it fogs, the interior mood is old cinema—the scenes playing on a black-and-white reel, except for the flower shop in the southeast corner, where sunflowers, tulips, calla lilies, roses, freesia, orchids, and begonia bloom beneath halo lights.

The snaking of lines. The impatient pacers. The phones to the ears, the cheekbones on duffel bags, the bodies curved before the novels just bought at Faber, and the heads thrown back against the benches. The chandeliers are creamy missiles. The voices echo inside the travertine walls—the Silver Star and the Silver Meteor are coming, the Cardinal and the Carolinian, the trains to Chicago and to Florida, to Boston, New York, and D.C.

Tickets out.
Line forms here.
All aboard.

And then, a rumble on the tracks below, a slight vibration felt in the waiting room above, a split-flap of the departure board, and it begins again.

Sometimes someone on the shoeshine throne. Sometimes spontaneous opera or ballroom dance or a job fair or a party. Sometimes a roving artist from the Porch at 30th—a BalletX boy or a Tangles acrobat or a master of cuisine carrying an extra slice of Di Bruno cheese. Sometimes a man on the *Forbes* "Richest People in America" list waits to exchange his ticket at the counter. He sees that he has been seen. He knows he won't be swarmed.

At the foot of the Pennsylvania Railroad World War II Memorial on the east end of the waiting room, the bronzed archangel Michael lifts a dying soldier from the consuming flames of war and hovers over the 1,307 names of those he could not save. In the north waiting room, where no one really waits, horses gallop out of Karl Bitter's stone and a child hurries ahead with the future in his hands. *The Spirit of Transportation*. Then.

If you are five feet tall, there are ninety feet of air between the top of your head and the coffered ceiling of the main waiting room. If you are among the pacers, you are polishing Tennessee marble with the soles of your shoes. If you are wondering about the past, you are wondering all the way back to the heart of the Depression, when Alfred Shaw of Graham, Anderson, Probst and White, a Chicago firm, persevered with his Art Deco obsession.

Shaw was to design a replacement for the old Broad Street Station as part of the city's beautification movement. He was to work through desperate years. He allowed himself to be inspired by the newish science of electricity, which enabled a separation of the trains and tracks from the waiting passengers. (No more soot on the suits, not in Philly.) He had ideas about the possibilities and responsibilities of train travel and incorporated, into an already monumental plan, pneumatic tube communications, a mortuary, a chapel, and more than three thousand square feet of hospital space.

The Chicagoan did what great architects do. Philadelphians did the rest.

Today, at Philadelphia's 30th Street Station, it is December. The big, lit tree is standing tall—no gimmick to it, a gentle appeal. The lines of people are skeins of yarn, the books at Faber are selling, the flowers at the stand are being coned into fat bouquets, the bags and the boxes and people go by, the suitcases on rollers, the hats and gloves. The steps go down and the escalators ride up, and in all this traffic of travel, in all the rumpus and pell-mell and fuss, all the yearning and pacing and dreaming, there is a private theater.

Our friends, our family, our people are coming home.

Indeed, there is a boy—a young man—out there on the rails. He smells (I know this already) of winter and the promise of snow. He carries with him gifts and stories—the gift, mostly, of story. He will surprise me, as he always does, with his height, with the quantity of light in the deep dark of his eyes, with his tenacity and sense of purpose.

He will surprise me, and then he will find me; he will hurry through the crowds. "I'm home," he'll say, and I'll be whole.

FRINGE WORK

DOUBLE DIPPING

Stone Harbor, New Jersey

In the same way that I believed in black raspberry ice cream, blue-fingered crab, and the pink sheen of a flipped shell, I believed, as a kid, in the Jersey Shore, specifically Stone Harbor. It possessed me and I possessed it those two weeks of every year when our parents would pack the caroming Oldsmobile with suits, rafts, shovels, pails, rusty-bottomed beach chairs, crab traps, tangled reels, and (where there was still room) my brother, my sister, and me.

We were only ever a couple of hours away—a big bridge and a few small ones. My father drove the back roads—farm country. We kept our windows down. We smelled ripening peaches and reddening tomatoes and kerneled corn long before we smelled the salt of the sea. Do white pebble lawns have a smell? How about the shallow wells of seaside miniature golf courses or the clogged heads of outside shower stalls or the tall grass that survives the sway of the dunes? I was sure that they did, and I was the first to call, "I smell it! Stone Harbor! We're here!"

The big events: Digging for clams with our toes and tossing the thick meat to the sudden stuttering of gulls above. Inflating the rafts until our faces were red. Lying on our backs in tidal pools, collecting freckles. Trapping crabs in the bay. Walking the froth line of the beach with our favorite uncle, who would come for one day, his trousers rolled to just below his knees. Choosing restaurants on the nights my mother didn't cook, and standing at the edge of the kitchen in the rented bungalow on the nights that she did, praying the newly imprisoned crabs (their claws in a rictus) would not escape their boiling pots. On rented bikes with clanging baskets we would make our way to town to spy on the hermit creatures with painted shells in the T-shirt store. In the morning, the sand of sleep still in our eyes, we'd wake to the doughnuts my father had scouted—two glazed with a touch of cream for me.

When it rained we'd play games and listen to the pebbled yards washing clean. When the sun was too hot, we cinched in beneath the Kephart umbrella and half slept, half dreamed. On the best night of the whole two weeks, we'd climb back into our Oldsmobile and drive to the bright lights and carousel cries of Ocean City. Am I the only one who remembers the caterpillar ride? The only one who remembers winning so big at Skee Ball that I emerged as a Springsteen-worthy queen?

Writing this now, I sorely miss then. It was sun before we suspected sun's poison and sweets before we felt the need to punish ourselves for delicious things. At Stone Harbor, we did what we wanted to do—explored or swam or walked or carved sculptures in the sand. I don't suppose we learned a thing we'd later use in school, but we were never learning at the beach. We were storing up particles of our future selves. We were conjuring then so that we'd have then for now.

And isn't that the point, indeed, when we find our mythic second home—that anywhere to which we longingly return in our imaginations until we can return for real? My Stone Harbor in August is, perhaps, his Poconos at dawn or her rooftop beneath a sheet of stars or his neighborhood pool after the dinner hour, when all but the most sweetly chlorinated have gone home. My Stone Harbor is my nostalgia. Outside of me, like all true fairy tales, it lives.

After my teenaged years—married, a mother—the Jersey Shore was lost to me. My Salvadoran husband preferred the high kick of the Pacific Ocean, and my father's beach had moved south, to the Carolinas. My brother is the one who brought Stone Harbor back— who began to rent a house just off of 96th Street as the summer wound down to its end. "Come for the day," he'd say, and I would— driving the highways because I couldn't find my father's back roads, and singing radio songs with my son.

In my middle age I do not own buckets, rafts, beach chairs, or traps. I've forgotten how to dig clams with my toes. I stink at miniature golf and my Skee Ball skills are rusty. But my brother and nephew have taught me the magic of beach bocce, and my niece talks about the books that she reads, and my sister-in-law allows her feet to be dug around and in between when they get in the way of a sand sculpture. In Stone Harbor, the summer ends, and I sit shielding my hair, face, and knees from the sun. I walk the frothy shore with my son. I take a book, but I dream instead.

At night, we head to Springer's Homemade Ice Cream over on 3rd Avenue and stand in line with the peeling crowd. I read every sumptuous flavor slowly—Almond Amaretto, Butterscotch Brickle, Cease and Desist, Mor*e*o, Prohibition Tradition, Springer Chip, Teaberry—and then I place my order. "A double scoop of black raspberry," I'll say. No one's surprised. Some fairy tales do not tolerate deviations.

FAMILY FOR THE DAY

Lancaster County

We had taken to the Sunday drive. Like shellfish appetizers on Christmas Eve or practical jokes before bedtime, it had come upon us like a family habit, a minor regularity within the everyday broil.

Our Jeep Wrangler was maligned by middle age. We had done little to correct the whorl of rattling parts, the foggy windows that flapped like bird wings. The brakes worked fine, and it was early fall, and the weather should have been mild. We had zippered off the plastic top—proof that we were fearless—and we were off to Amish country.

I wore two jackets and stuffed my hands between my knees. My husband blasted the neighborhood with the unmighty Wrangler heater. Our son, behind us, secured his seat belt like a trooper, though his fingers, chalky white, were slowly freezing. The sky was opaque on one side, bare blue on the other. Surely the sun was coming.

The trappings of suburbia began to fall away. We made our way from where we lived to that part of Pennsylvania where the towns go by names like Bird-in-Hand, Paradise, and Intercourse and the homes are lit by naphtha lanterns, and the land stretches gold and green beneath the hoofs of patient animals. We drove a route of garish signs and service stations, navigated a knot of retail malls, jeeped across a stretch of six-lane highway, and bisected a ribbon of mobile homes and roadside ranchers until time tocked to a different tempo.

We slowed for the horse-drawn carriage, the black-cab gleam, the horse trot. We looked for the stubble of new crops, the steam of manure, the distances and expanse of things. We kept on jeeping. Saw a boy in barn-door britches and flat-crowned hat scooting his way down the road on a pair of skates. Saw a cluster of girls in white organdy aprons and dark button-and-hook dresses sharing pious secrets behind their hands. Saw old men in black suit coats and unmarred beards in a solemn circle on the stoop of a church, and also the women in their separate circle, their hair rolled into sheer prayer caps. We were intruders obeying the infrequent traffic signs and looking (for it was still so cold) for shelter.

We'd already passed Good and Plenty. We'd let Good Food go by. We'd come upon Fancy Farms. We parked in the black lake of newly painted asphalt and made a stumbling run for the restaurant door, the wind whipping our stiff joints around until we doubled over with what was either laughter or pain. We yanked open the door and we thought that this perhaps was Paradise—four walls, a roof, the nudge of heated air.

We were not accustomed to the restaurant set-up; we were told that we must pay before we eat. We couldn't even see the tables from where we stood, and we didn't know what we were buying, but never mind. It was warm inside. We surrendered our money, congratulated ourselves on our choice.

Now we headed through the lobby and around the corner, a family of three on its way to an intimate lunch. But when the dining room came into view I saw a communal picnic instead—long rectangular tables dressed in plastic checkered cloths, corrugated pitchers of water pinning the tablecloths down, patrons gathered around a single table passing cinnamon bread in a basket and sipping iced water from blue mugs. This, the trainee gestured, was our table.

I politely suggested that one of the empty tables might do.

I was leveled by a look somewhere between righteous and indignant. "This," she said, "is your family for the day."

Rules being rules, we took our seats. Manners being manners, we attended to the introductions. "I'm South Carolina," the woman beside my husband said. "I'm Virginia," the woman beside South Carolina said. "I'm South Carolina but related to Virginia," the man beside her said.

"We're Pennsylvania," I declared.

Please pass the butter.

The waiter appeared with instructions about the fare. Roast beef, fried chicken, beans, mashed potatoes. A new family wandered in, joined us, and soon enough the plates were coming and we were passing and scooping, and every once in a while someone said something almost funny until a conversation stirred. Miss Virginia was recently widowed, she said. Mr. South Carolina was her brother-in-law. Mrs. South Carolina was a grandmother and she had a necklace full of children charms to show.

Sometime during second helpings, the table perked with causerie. Mr. and Mrs. South Carolina recounted their life of peregrination. Miss Virginia recalled the sunsets of Juneau. The newest among us spoke fondly of their eldest, who was teaching islanders English far from home. I was sitting in the middle and therefore privy to all matters, and every once in a while, when things spiraled downward, I asked a question or I raised a palm or I said, "Miss Virginia, that's a keeper." After a while, Mr. South Carolina dubbed me the party monger, the picnic-table hinge.

Isn't it strange? I sat there thinking. Isn't it odd, our makeshift party? I didn't even know my compatriots' given names, but we were, in fact, a sudden family. Thrown upon each other, we had obeyed the spoken rules, we had touched one another, passed the fare. We'd listened, confided, dreamed out loud, and now Mr. South Carolina was saying that his missus is a bugger, and Miss Virginia was saying that the lonely nights get stale, and the newest among us admitted to nerves on cooking day. What has happened here? I wanted to ask, but the clock was ticking, and the shoofly pie was gone, and the waiter came to tell us that the tip was separate from the bill. Now, as we scrounged in our pockets for bills, we looked for excuses to prolong our masquerade. We asked each other questions more intently, wished each other well, hoped for glorious birthdays for one and less loneliness for the other and a very fine rest of the day in the land of Paradise.

LOST AND FOUND

Glenside

Still standing:

- The house we bought when we left the city—its well-shaded porch and its boxed-in backyard, its hairy hedge, the colors that we eventually made it (Cape May colors in rebellion against gray), its flip-top mailbox into which and out of which came word of my future in publishing. Letters typed out and signed. *Iowa Woman* says yes. So do the *Sonora Review, Alaska Quarterly,* the *Crescent Review, Northeast Quarterly,* and *Literal Latte,* but not the *New Yorker,* never the *New Yorker,* and also that perpetual "almost" from *The Atlantic* that is in fact a permanent no.
- Humphrey's Pest Control and its petrified roaches, termites, carpet beetles, its storefront proof of the coming plague.
- The neighbor who tucked encouragement into cakes, who trimmed the hedge, who lent me her children.
- The train station where I stood most evenings with my young son, waving goodbye, then hello. *Here comes the train.* The railroad

tracks, like a prostrate ladder. The sound of the train, the endless sound of the train, set your clocks by it, count the times.

• The Elizabethan Keswick Theatre and its ornamental plasters, that white-and-gold tickled organ, those seats where we sat in the audience of them: Leonard Cohen, Joan Armatrading, the Roche sisters, Dan Fogelberg. Third row, to the right. Back row, just in time. Our history in song.

• The hills we walked. The bakery we ate in. The fence along the schoolyard where we stood, leaning and listening for the changes in the seasons. The library and the Harley shop (we stopped to read the signs; we stopped to look). The basement in the church that was his school.

• The porch where we stood, saying goodbye.

Remembered:

• Rizzo's Pizza.
• The nest I found with the pair of robins.
• The poem I wrote for the borrowed children:

> *You had expected the pain*
> *Of a dam breaking*
> *Or a cork ripping free,*
> *And so you did not cry when it came*
> *In new blood on a string—*
> *A dangerous dangle*
> *Above the sink. You brought the news*
>
> *Through the hole in your grin. . . .*

• The second-hand store where I bought the rocking chair that made me (just days before the birth of my son) a verifiable mother.
• The Christmas party at Mrs. Wheatland's house: *Here, she said, you'll need some jingle bells.*

- The nurse next door who terrified every October 31st—leaping from the dark, masked, screaming to the ends of the earth, and I watched him, and I saw it coming, and I was frightened, too.
- The flowers I bought to console myself.
- The swan-footed couch, the turtle sandbox, the Venetian masks, the attic dolls, the hook from which we hung the piñata, the candy that fell.
- The children who disappeared from childhood.
- The idea of who I was.

What I didn't see coming:

- The ferocious altitudes of love.
- The generative power of yes.
- The patterns that became responsibilities, the responsibilities that became a life, the idea that became a memory, the idea that was superseded.
- The accretion of time, my face in the mirror, the boy now taller than I am, the way we walk together, still, the way walking became our history, is our history, is us, moving ahead.
- The nostalgia I feel for the Cape May colors, the flip-top mail, the piñata candy, long-gone birds, the silken weight of a child in my arms, the things we left.

So that we say:

- We were young there.
- We were young once.

RIVER ROAD

New Hope and the Delaware River

I'll take my Schuylkill River wherever I can find her. In the shadows
of the South Street Bridge. At the bend by Bartram's Garden. Along
the edge of Venice Island. Beneath the angled trees of Pottstown. In
the dark green hush of Hamburg.

To contemplate the Delaware River I like to travel north—past
Yardley and Washington Crossing, to New Hope, Centre Bridge,
Lumberville, Erwinna, Upper Black Eddy. Route 32. River Road.

It's not that I don't appreciate the Delaware River's Philadelphia history—the captains and riggers and cave dwellers, the flotilla
of trading schooners, the congested mercantile culture that broke
Thomas Holme's orderly grid, the pirates and the freebooters, the
whales. It's not that I haven't sat for long spells at Penn's Landing
or walked the tight streets or pondered Camden from Philadelphia's
eastern edge.

It's that I like the way River Road winds. I like how it becomes,
over the passing miles, an egress, a parade, a retreat. River Road is a
going-somewhere road. It has a sense of purpose.

You drive and it winds. You take note: George Washington was here, Christmas 1776, his men breaking the ice with their paddles and his musicians carrying muskets. You see pumpkins in October and blooms in spring, and it's especially pretty after a night of snow when the sun yellows through the ice-tipped trees.

At the southern edge of New Hope, the parade begins. The long line of convertible Honda 2000s, red-leather backed and open to the sky. The choppers and cruisers and touring bikes, the helmet heads and bandanas. The kids in striped socks. The tourists with maps. The glimpse of a towpath to the west, the Bucks County Playhouse to the right, the Celtic traders and (Dough) Nation and the year-round Christmas hut. The art beside the hippie shops. Logan Inn.

Your car is going nowhere fast. You have become the spectacle.

Then, past the bridge to Lambertville (two hundred years old and standing), past Topeo One and Topeo Two, past Mother's Restaurant, the congestion eases and River Road runs out ahead. The homes along the Delaware are tenacious—some clawed into place like characters from a Tolkien book, some bulwarked with modern-day defenses. The river, it seems, always wins. The architecture cranks toward and honors it. The contours of the horse farms and the stone outcroppings, the estates like empires, the houses that sit as close as houses dare, for there will be storms, there will be floods, there will be damage here.

It's worth getting out in Lumberville, where the sandwiches at the General Store are rustic and the sweets are worth packing for a picnic farther on. It's worth ambling over the Raven Rock Bridge to the sycamore and silver maple of Bull's Island. It's a Roebling bridge, multi-catenary and suspended. You leave one state. You enter another. You get back in the car and drive on.

Over wine at the Centre Bridge Inn, my husband and I decided: Let's have a child. Over a feast at an Erwinna inn, we celebrated my mother. At the Bridgeton House on the Delaware, we retreated for Thanksgiving—walked across the Delaware into New Jersey and back, again, then sat down for pheasant instead of turkey. I've walked the towpath of Lambertville beside a famous poet, hunting for snowdrops. I've been caught in a small cyclone of lemon-colored leaves in Tinicum Park. I bought a green-glass seahorse in Topeo, a commitment ring from the Celtic shop, a chocolate chip cookie from the Lumberville General Store that never got past the parking lot.

I have wondered, every time I've driven through, what it would be like to live along or near this River Road, beside this swath of the Delaware's hundreds of miles, beside tributary histories and Tolkein architecture.

I have wondered, then I have driven home.

GARDEN RETREAT IN
THE HIGH HEAT OF SUMMER

Chanticleer Garden

Some one hundred million years ago, according to Loren Eiseley, the great anthropologist and Penn professor, the world was monochrome green. No dahlia, no foxglove, no halo-headed hydrangea, no speckled lily. Continent by continent, flowerlessness reigned. Dinosaurs dreamed in forest hues.

And then, Eiseley writes in *How Flowers Changed the World*, "just a short time before the close of the Age of Reptiles, there occurred a soundless, violent explosion." The explosion was color and fruit, pistils and stamen. It was the stuff of what would become and now remains our very lives—energy, oxygen, seeds.

We tend to forget, all these millennia later, that flowers aren't merely holiday bromides and that gardens aren't just imperfectly containered art. Flowers and therefore gardens are the place where things begin and then, inevitably, cycle through: seedlings, sprouts, stalks, blooms, and finally, quietly, stardust.

We need gardens to remind ourselves of who and what we are, of what evanescent means, of myth and metaphor. We need them especially in these lamentably hot summer days, when asphalt burns and the sun is a weight against the skin and our thoughts grow gauzy, suffused. We need the rejuvenating kick of a breeze over a running stream, the shadowy reprieve beneath a tree, the bright light of monarch wings, the cautionary float of lotus pink on ponds. We need gardeners who don't give up beneath stingy clouds. We need to place our faith in wells.

Walk a garden and the temperature cools. Walk a garden, and a bird will sing to you. Walk a garden, and much of what you suspect is true will be returned to you. That you are of this world, but it does not belong to you. That you are temporary here. That if you want to use your earth time well, you best make room for beauty.

Philadelphia, that green country town, is garden rich—big and small, urban and rural, more or less tame. It's home to the nation's oldest still-thriving botanical garden in the country (Bartram's Garden), a menagerie of college gardens, a garden called Wyck, a garden called Grumblethrope, and 650 acres' worth of shade (Tyler Arboretum). My garden of proximity and choice is Chanticleer—nearly forty acres of botanical theater and pleasure located in the town of Wayne.

I discovered Chanticleer a dozen years ago when I was prematurely gnarled—my jaw tight, my muscles rigid, my hours overburdened with responsibilities. I had written too many books, or thought I had, and I wanted to live, for a spell, without the measure of words. I wanted to stand straight and walk far, or to sit still and see. I wanted to spend my time doing absurdly useless things like wonder where the dragonfly goes or how the bird builds her nest or what the turtle in the swamp thinks all day.

Chanticleer was literature of a new kind, history found not in books but in the minor accelerations of hills and the unpretentious wending of water. It was the lessons of the gardeners who took time to answer questions and who taught me something about seeding, staking, dividing, and letting go.

I ultimately wrote two books—one a memoir, one a novel for young adults—based on my love for this garden. I taught inner-city and suburban kids about writing against Chanticleer's backdrop. And when my mother died, I placed a memorial to her at Chanticleer in the form of an engraved stone that now sits beneath the two great katsura trees. A gardener fit that stone snugly in. He judged the sun and how it fell to give that stone its proper eternal home.

In the high heat of this summer I find myself again returning to Chanticleer—walking the garden alone or with friends. The sunflowers, gladiola, and hollyhocks are tall in the cutting garden. The water cascades (a clean sheet of cool) over the stone faces of the ruins and sits in a black hush in the sarcophagus. Bursts of color illuminate the dark shade of the Asian Woods. The creek runs thin but determined.

I don't know why I am forever surprised by all this. I don't know how it is that a garden I know so well—its hills, its people, its tendencies, its blocks of shade—continues to startle me, to teach me, to remind me about the sweet, cheap thrill of unbusyness, say, or the impossibility of perfect control. We do not commandeer nature—gardeners know this best of all. We are born of it, live with it, are destined for return.

Dust to dust, yes. But why not shade and blooms in between? Why not gardens in this summer of infernal, angry heat?

ON A WING AND A PRAYER

Hawk Mountain

This is the way a raptor flies: north to south from August through December, south to north in April and May. Coasting on deflected winds when she can, cresting on the lift of thermals, hunting down voles and mice and toads, sometimes finishing her meal in the sky. Every year millions of hawks, eagles, and falcons fill the skies above North America. And every year we look up and wonder. We are earthbound. They are soaring.

Early one morning years ago, I made the hour-and-a-half trek to Hawk Mountain Sanctuary, the oldest such sanctuary in the country and keeper of the longest record of raptor migrations. It was one of those effulgent days, when everything seemed touched by the intimation of precious metal—platinum on the limbs of trees, silver in the tips of flowers, gold glinting off weathervanes. By the time I hit Hawk Mountain Road, the landscape was storybook: Big red barns. Horses gathered near a river. White silos. Wide swaths of green.

The road bent and rose. I passed a sign marking the Appalachian Trail—Maine in one direction, and Georgia in the other—a reminder that Hawk Mountain sits on the three-hundred-mile-long Kittatinny Ridge, straddling Schuylkill and Berks Counties. I turned onto a gravel road. I was alone. In the silence I heard the call of birds.

Hawk Mountain Sanctuary is twenty-six hundred acres wide and, at its highest, fifteen hundred feet tall. It is eight miles of trails ranging from the flat and smooth to steep and rocky. I headed off to South Lookout, a terrace built of sandstone boulders, and stopped. There, below, was the River of Rocks, a relic from the most recent Ice Age. Rising among the fifteen-thousand-year-old rocks were oaks and a scattering of pine.

It helps to be quiet, while waiting for birds. For the buteos and the red-tailed hawk, the broad-winged hawk, the accipiters, the sharp-shinned hawk, and the northern goshawk, the peregrine falcon and the American kestrel, the sacred bald eagle. I waited for these, but it was a turkey vulture that I saw, holding its wings in a V, bobbing and tipping, rising on an ascending spiral. It was self-assured and magnificently practiced in the aerodynamics of flight, hunting for signs of death in the valley.

I wanted to fly, too. I wanted wind rush and intimacy with weather, eyes that acutely see, a body attuned to the physics of lift and weight, thrust and drag. I wanted wings and feathers, I wanted more birds, and so I kept walking. Up the hill, past mountain laurel and mountain ash, clumps of rhododendron, chestnut, maple, and oak trees, the flit of bird song. By the time I reached North Lookout, I had climbed several hundred feet in elevation and had ascended a steep stairway of uneven sandstone.

I stood with kicked-up Ice Age stone and a few stumpy mountain ash trees growing out of thin soil. There was nothing between me and the earth below but other lovers of raptors, with their binoculars and wind gauges, their caps and burnished skin. I chose a rock, settled in, and looked out from that great height. The trees beyond were leaves and color. The valley was an emerald green. I had sky on my skin, and sun.

"Three broad-wingeds, two ospreys, two red-tail, one sharp-shin," someone said, reporting the day's bounty, the birds that had flown overhead while I had been down among the laurel, climbing.

"Nothing for a while," another said.

"Slow morning."

"No eagles."

But something would be soaring soon, and so I sat there. Waiting.

HEART ON THE HORSES

The Devon Horse Show and Country Fair

The township men pound the No Parking signs in with the cheek of a hammer, and that's how we know the horses are coming. The international jumpers. The long-tailed Friesians. The high-stepping roadsters. The disciplined saddlebreds. The hunters. The cobtails. The paraphernalia of carriages, curry brushes, ribbons, saddles, reins, harnesses, and whips. The riders, the trainers, the crews, the farriers. The *equestrians.*

They come every year—a ten-day carnival—and we, the neighbors and near-neighbors of the Devon Horse Show and Country Fair, decide. Either we'll pimp out our lawns as grassy parking lots (ten dollars a spot), or we'll not. The choice is ours.

Some people buy their houses to secure access to a certain school or proximity to a particular landscape—topographical, social, or otherwise. Nearly twenty years ago, when my family of three was on the hunt for a house, I had my heart set on the horses. I remembered Memorial Day weekends from decades before, when my father, mother, brother, sister, and I would make the drive to the leafy streets of Devon, Pennsylvania. We'd park along a distant curve (these were the pre-sign days), walk the hill, buy our tickets, pass through the threshold of the milky blue-and-white gates, and there it all lay— the white sands of the Dixon Oval, the amiable grandstands, the crunchy paths, the candy spreads, the knick-knack shops, the Pulitzer colors, the stalls, the fairgrounds.

At the rails we'd suck our lemon sticks and watch the igloos of our ice cream melt. On the Midway, we'd wait in line for the Ferris wheel, throw darts into balloons, walk around with our hairy, polyester prizes (a monkey, I think I remember, maybe a frog). Between events, or seeking shade, we'd drift back to the stables, where trainers would sit on cubes of straw and dogs would curl into the leather backs of grounded saddles and mothers would pin bows into the shellacked hair of tiny riders. We'd choose our favorite horses and cheer them on, and when night came, we'd trail through the gates and down the streets, the announcer's voice following us as we walked beneath the stars. We could hear him still announcing ponies as we began the drive home.

I had my heart set, and we bought the house. It was small and old, right enough.

I'm not the only one who has built a life around this show. In fact, the whole thing was set in motion more than 115 years ago when a "Meeting of the Gentlemen" inaugurated a single-day fair on the grounds of the enormous Devon Inn, where the city's elite went to enjoy the spring-fed lakes, polo, racing, dancing, theater, and meals sourced by the inn's own farm. The Gentlemen had in mind an educational event—a demonstration of fine harness horses, a conversation about breeding. They conducted their business on the inn's racetrack and polo field, where the grounds remain today.

By 1919 a country fair was being held in association with the show and Bryn Mawr Hospital was the official beneficiary. No show has ever rivaled Devon's, according to the show's own press. Today it remains "the largest outdoor horse show in the country"—raising millions for the hospital, rewarding the winners, and attracting

Olympic riders, the daughters of rock stars, reality TV celebrities, and a surfeit of women in hats.

I don't own a hat, and with my unkempt curls, my frayed-at-the-hems jeans, my wilderness garden, and my unorthodox literary ways, I'm hardly Main Line material. I don't even know that much about horses, to be honest; I just know how much I love to be around them—the smell of them, the heat that flares from their nostrils, the large disks of their eyes, the flicker of their tails, the quiet in the stalls. I love the horses, the tradition that carries on.

So the No Parking signs go in, and the horses in their trailers come, and I live here now—leaving the house early those ten days of the show and heading down toward the newest fleet of stables, where the hunters and jumpers and show ponies are. A farrier will show me how to fit a horse into shoes. A mane will get braided. The dogs will lie languid, and across the street, in the fairgrounds proper, thousands of volunteers will open shops, test mikes, sort ribbons, get the hot dogs going on.

We bought the house. I still believe in the show.

I THOUGHT I COULD DANCE

Ardmore

How I stood, how I sat, how I walked into a room and didn't possess it—these were concerns. Also: the untamed wilderness of my hair, but we would get to that. In addition: the way I hid behind my clothes and failed their easy angles. Most troubling, perhaps: my tendency to rush, my feverish impatience with myself, my heretofore undiagnosed problem with the art of being led.

So I thought I could dance.

So I imagined the ballroom instructors leaning in to say—first rumba or perhaps the second—*You've got a knack for this.*

What knack? What had I done? Why had I not realized that dancing in the dark alone to Bruce Springsteen does not qualify anyone for the cha-cha? That grace is not necessarily an elevated pointer finger? That how they do it on TV is how they do it on TV? That loving to dance does not a dancer make you?

Still, for years now I have been climbing the narrow staircase to the second-floor studio of DanceSport Academy in Ardmore, looking out on the changing scene of party shops, travel agencies, and olive oil sellers, and taking my place on worn floorboards. I have submitted to assessments, acquiesced to leaders, persisted among the surround-sound of reflective glass, danced with my husband and danced without him, and learned more from a gorgeous twelve-year-old girl than I would ever be able to teach her. I have New Yorkered, ganchoed, promenaded, ronde chassed, rocked left, rocked right, shined, forward progressed. I have confessed my deepest fears, sheared off polished toenails, neglected my actual profession, chopped my hair and grown it back, begged for mercy, philosophized, caught my breath, and in between—it has happened so slowly—I have jived, tangoed, mamboed, fox trotted, risen and fallen again.

I have done this while the cars of Lancaster Avenue have gone east and west below. I have done it while watching the crowds gather for a guitar jam at the nearby coffee shop. While watching ladies knit in the shop across the street. I have stood at the banded windows looking out on the world going by, and then I have stepped onto that floor and danced.

Don't want so much, I have been told, but also: *Want more deeply. Learn the steps so that you can forget them,* the instructors have said, immune to their own contradictions. *Listen to the music,* they've implored me, and then they've counted: *One-and-ah-two-and-AHHHH-three. Make it smaller, bigger, better, tighter, looser. Where's your control?* they've exclaimed, hiding their own frustrations— mostly. In their English-as-a-second-language way, my instructors have *regarded* me. For forty-five minutes each lesson, they have set me free to fail and free to try again, and in the process I have learned a little something about my own tenacity and hurt, my multiform needs. I have, as well, made some of my most enduring friends, and once I sat beside my mother in a hospital room, showing her a video of me trying.

"Wow," she said, one of her final words to me. *Wow.* Because her daughter was standing a little taller than before. Because her daughter, for a few ephemeral moments in a long tomboy life, had at last tamed her hair.

If you doubt the intelligence of dance, watch real dancers. See what they prove about the possible. See how they thrive in three-dimensional space. See how full of the vivid they are. Dance may be a thin line of knowing and a strange untelling of song, it may be theater, but in ballroom anyway, dance is also a conversation with a single, striving other. He moves and she reacts. He suggests, and she adorns. They, together, forsake words in favor of something even more primal and true. Dancing is muscle and mood and moxie, and can you blame me for wanting it still, through all these years? Can you blame me for heading back up those stairs, week upon week— bloodied, battered, yearning, determined to get my body right, to know it more completely, to be an equal, trusted partner in the dialogue of dance?

I'm still getting more wrong than right, still disappointed with my arms, still trying to talk some more consistent sense into my hair, still a disaster in the sequins department. Nonetheless, when the showcase events come around—when I, an aspirant member of the DanceSport Academy community, head to the stage of area auditoriums in Haverford, Villanova, Radnor, or Bryn Mawr—I am striving, I am hoping to be intelligent with sound. I am believing that Cher and Christina and Robin Thicke will speak to me while I dance with my husband of Latin hips.

And so the lights go up. And the music starts. And a couple hundred people in the chairs beyond me wait. I dance, I fail, but what is failure, really? Not trying, not yearning, not risking, perhaps. I'll fail until this body stops me.

ACCIDENTAL TOURISTS

Wilmington, Delaware

We were refugees—two among hundreds of thousands in the sudden snap of cold and dark. We had listened to the savaging of trees, the terrible torque and release of high-up limbs. We had feared for our rooftops, our abandoned cars, the iced utility lines that hung like glassy staffs between tilting poles. We had succumbed to the dissipation of heat and waited for trains that did not run and there was the sound of sirens farther on—trouble that far exceeded ours.

February 5, 2014. The ice storm had come.

We drove the dystopian landscape looking for proof that help was on its way. We listened to generators jabber and groan like so many old secrets, watched smoke huff through chimney stacks, wondered about the birds and how far they'd flown. We pitied the jack-knifed trees, the bushes iced to the ground, the power lines that had been indiscriminately flung over buried gardens, sidewalks, roads. We took shelter on streets miraculous with power, in the still-percolated coffee shops, over communal power strips, and one day went by, and then two, and family by family, we had to choose.

When our house filled with smoke after a misbegotten fireplace fire, we packed our bags for Wilmington. Forty minutes later, we arrived to a hushed mid-afternoon. Trailing ashes, still warming our hands, we checked into a small Delaware Avenue hotel, and soon set out by foot to explore Delaware's largest city and New Castle County's county seat.

How many times had we passed her by on our way down I-95, toward more distant southern climes? How often had we looked up from our seats on the Amtrak train and wondered about the city that lay beyond the rails? Now here we were, walking Rodney Square and organizing the buildings in our mind—classical revival, Beaux-Arts, contemporary. We stood beneath the towering steeple of First and Central Church. We entered the lobby of the grand Hotel DuPont, 101 years old and full of flourish. We followed the sloping streets to the broad arm of the Christina River and whatever lay beyond her.

There was no ice to speak of, no hurry. The only crowd was the bus-stop queue. There was a glow in the faces of old buildings, spots of sun on a tower, light in the broad windows of the public library. Accidental tourists with neither map nor plan, we circled and walked on.

There are countless ways to come to know a city. I prefer—a novelist's bad habit—to imagine my way in, collecting feelings ahead of facts. I talk to the people who will talk to me. I eavesdrop on the everyday. I pay attention to the places that I, in another lifetime, might decide to call my own.

In Wilmington, we discovered the exuberantly restored Grand (Opera House) scrubbed into a shine. We nodded to the Queen, now home of WXPN Café Live. We stopped inside the quiet parenthesis of Willington Square—a "representative" courtyard of mid-eighteenth-century brick houses that had been uprooted and relocated to suggest the city's mercantile past. We headed to the train station, the Tubman-Garrett Riverfront Park, and (again) the Christina herself and all that has been set down beside her. The Penn Cinema. The Chase Center. The Delaware Center for the Contemporary Arts. The Delaware Theatre Company. Restaurants. A collection of painted bird houses sit along the river walk—fanciful, inviting. The old stuff of the city's shipbuilding past has been restored. And in the riverfront market—a revitalized warehouse built of thick walls and massive timbers—the commerce of the day was getting done.

We had found, during our meanderings, a restaurant on Market Street called La Fia Bakery + Market + Bistro—tin ceilings, light wood, big windows, an easy, unpretentious storefront. We returned that night for a meal. Nothing was playing at either the Grand or the Queen, and so the server had time to answer questions. The poached salmon with the crème fraîche was a favorite, he said. The grilled octopus was very nice. The mural above the bar was painted by the owner-chef, whose name, it became clear, is Bryan Sikora, once of Philadelphia's own Django and a.kitchen. La Fia had opened in mid-2013, we were told. People came from all across the country just to try the lamb.

We ordered dessert.

The next night we found Market Street crowded with cars and alive with artists and the people who support them, which is to say: We found the people of Wilmington. A high-school talent show playing at the Queen. An exhibit of art by bird preservationists at the library. A concoction of artists—photographers, sculptors, painters—at the Delaware College of Art and Design. We wandered in and out and listened. In a city famous for setting so many free, we were not turned away. We were alerted, most of all, to the hospitality of a place as forty minutes north the nights stayed dark and the air was cold, but help was finally on its way.

SKYTOP LODGE

The Poconos

Sometime in my late childhood, Skytop became a family tradition. We'd leave at dusk on a Friday in February and drive the highways until we reached the narrow roads, the towns with names like Mountainhome and Cresco, the sudden press of dark, suggestive beauty. By the time we'd entered Canadensis, we were driving slowly, watching for deer and the occasional roadside attraction, hunting for the break in the evergreens and the sign, the famous Skytop sign, encased as it always was that time of year in long, swanning cords of ice made amber by the flood lights. Skytop was our winter, where snow was tame and ice was sculpture, where the same bellhops greeted us year after year, as if we'd been absent only a brief while.

We'd spend the first night in the frigid air on the old toboggan run—soaring out across the frozen lake, hollering our heroics to anyone who'd listen. Only when we were impenetrably numb would we retreat to the lodge, huddle before its fireplace, and thaw, heading downstairs, in time, to the Ping-Pong tables, the pool room, the coffee shop, the mild rivalries of other February weekend guests.

We'd see the same families the next day in the huge dining room at breakfast, where decorum was mostly maintained over white tablecloths and halved grapefruits, oatmeal, granola, raisins, eggs, so many silver pots of hot chocolate. We'd see them on the hayrides and at the outdoor picnics, on the seven thousand feet of downhill slopes or the fifteen miles of cross-country skiing, in their snowshoes or their snow tubes, at the weather-protected skating rink. I learned to ski at Skytop. I met my first true boyfriend there. I went farther than anyone else I know across that lake on that splintered toboggan. And then our family grew up, and we stopped going to Skytop, and we hardly spoke of it again.

Twenty-five years went by before I returned to Skytop. I went in December, not February. I went with my husband and my son, the one that native Salvadoran, the other the sort of kid who has only ever appreciated snow for its power to shut down school on a test day. I went not knowing how much the place might have changed, whether it was ever all my memory made it, whether this childhood tradition would survive so many years.

We left at noon on Christmas day, arrived some time near two. *Look for the sign,* I said, after we'd passed Canadensis, and three miles later there it was, encased in ice. And there, too, was Skytop itself—more graceful than I'd remembered, and somehow larger, too, its stone façade glinting aura colors in the sun that was reflected off the snow. I remembered the bellhop who helped us from the car. He pretended that he remembered me. We were too late for the Christmas dinner, but they served us anyway—setting us down in the nearly empty dining room, bringing us lamb, shrimp, crab, green beans, and potatoes, delivering two desserts each at the end of the meal in the spirit of the season.

This generosity, I would soon be reminded, is typical Skytop, where the meals are always served in alarmingly large portions and the inn is packed with endless distractions (an indoor pool, a health club, spa facilities, a library, movies and concerts for the kids) and the grounds themselves go on and on, offering an ice-skating rink, ski slopes, nature trails, and, in the summer, golf, skeet shooting, tennis, lawn bowling, archery, bicycling, and the Orvis Fly Fishing school. Our room was upstairs—two windows offering views of the golf course and the bowling lawn, both obscured by snow. We changed into double layers and set off for the toboggan run, which we found easily enough—found it abandoned. The lake ice was no longer reliable, it seemed, and hadn't been for years, and so we walked past it, along the snowy shore of Skytop Lake, taking in the views that kept changing with the light. By the time we circled the lake and reached the lodge, the sun was gone, the guests were finishing their tea, the white-haired piano player was one song away from quits, though the teenaged guest who was singing with her was clearly angling for more show time.

The next day we set off for the trails. Some thirty miles' worth loop across Skytop's fifty-five hundred acres—thirty miles of increasingly challenging hikes that lead to glacial bogs and hemlock gorges, beaver marshes and antique forests, to the evidence of porcupine, coyote, bobcat mink, otter, black bear. The Lenni-Lenape hunted, fought, made love in Skytop acreage some eight thousand years before Christ was born; and long before the Indians settled, the mountain hummocks that cradle Skytop were folded earth beneath the sea, encrusted coral reefs.

Between evergreens and rhododendrons, oak and maple trees, we made our way to the Indian Ladder Falls, the most beautiful in all Pennsylvania, or so said the writer Wallace Nutting. I don't know what they look like unfrozen, but frozen, as we found them that day, the Ladder Falls were wedged between red rocks and trees, backlit by a cloudless sky, the falls themselves trapped into white fringes of exuberant ice, like so much vanilla frosting on the side of a cake. We left to climb Pocono Mountain, my son far out in front, his snowprints the only snowprints between his boots and ours. From the top of Pocono Mountain you can turn and face the lodge, see how doll-like it seems from such a distance. You can imagine it in spring—lush with wildflowers, little coteries headed out to the links, to the tennis courts, to the archery and the lawn bowling greens, to the lakes and streams swollen with sunfish, perch, and pickerel. You can stand and imagine as well the glaciers that once welled in the distance of the weathered mountain peak, imagine the Indians, then the industrialists, then the investors, then Skytop's founders themselves looking out across the land and deciding how best to make use of so much beauty.

At the height of the Roaring Twenties, four men set out to create a place that would offer respite to its patrons—clean air, long walks, stocked streams, fine sports, massages, books, the grace of a muted sun on a long, well-furnished porch, family-style meals. It was a club at first, for members only, and it would survive the Great Depression when so many other hotels failed. It would survive, it would be expanded, it would acquire a national reputation, and so many families would make it their own—get acquainted with the bellhops, seize the win at Ping-Pong, soar across the ice on a sled beneath a pregnant moon, pass down the ghost tales that haunt the hemlocked ravine of Devil's Hole. Skytop was always, has always been extravagant, and yet, somehow, it has always been about families, too—about girls who find first boyfriends on the slopes, about boys and their fathers who learn at last to love the snow.

AFTER THE STORM

Beach Haven, New Jersey, Pre-season

Beach Haven, Long Beach Island: pre-season.

The blades of dolphin fins at dawn: jeweled and slivered.

The locals packing the bar at Buckalew's.

A handful of teens counting down a friendly wrestling match by the shore.

One solitary kite kicked up over the sea foam.

A father and a son and a yellow Lab race outlaw skateboards on the tennis courts, where the nets are not yet hung, and the hardy clientele have gathered at the windswept Sand Bar, and at the island's southern end, at the wildlife preserve, one man in a parked car watches the frothy waves roll in.

The soup is on at Country Kettle Chowda. There are free chunks of Kettle fudge over *there*. The cures and conveniences of Kapler's Pharmacy are for sale on brighter shelves, and Murphy's Marketplace glimmers, and the restored door is open at How to Live—the loose fashion and garden ornaments and simplicity cards causing a stir among the handful of female shoppers.

Also: the pigs are scrubbed at Uncle Will's Pancake House, and the coffee's fresh, and they are doing up the French toast as they always have—quick and confectioner's sugar stylish. Also: the Saturday night wait is on at the Black Whale, the seafood specials impermanently inked onto the board. There are costumes hanging on a rack in the back of the Surflight Theatre, dogs off their leashes in the dog park, and over on Dock Street, the New Jersey Maritime Museum has got on a fresh coat of spearmint-tinted paint, while inside, its four hundred notebooks of history, its rescued china platters, its shipwreck artifacts, its speaking trumpet, its old postcards are all, mercifully, intact, as is Deborah C. Whitcraft, not just the museum's bold leader, not just an EMT but the mayor emeritus and a wedding officiant and one of the best storytellers Beach Haven has.

Dusk still turns out the lights over the bay. The oystercatchers still dazzle with their stop-sign red bills. The northern harriers still ride the thermals, the buffleheads still dive, and I suspect there'll always be that hint of gold in the deep of the big gulls' eyes.

It won't be long now before they take the wraps off at the Giant Wheel and the Sea Dragon at Fantasy Island. Not long before they open for service at the Marlin or before the bustle begins in the shipyards, and in the Craftmarket, and up and down the wide main street. For real. In earnest. Again.

There are new grasses in newly heaped dunes.

There is fresh wood along the docks.

There is life diversifying in the salt-marsh islands.

There is the sound of hammers and drills, electric sanders and industrial staplers where the rebuilding goes on and on.

All these months after Superstorm Sandy aimed its massive eye at our eastern shore—after many were forced to leave the homes they loved, the schools they taught in, the motels they managed, the restaurants where there was always sufficient sweet sugar and cold-enough beer—spring has come on, which means summer will be soon. The long lines on the bridge. The bright bikinis and the over-large towels. The ice cream melting over the cones. The shows that must go on.

Those of us who remember (and who doesn't remember?) the poststorm photographs—the evacuation trucks on the boulevards, the houses on their suddenly exposed stilts, the sand knee deep down the main streets, the trailer homes like bumper cars, the boats adrift; the stuff of the original Hand's Store ("If Hands doesn't have it; you don't need it.") tossed and torn and saturated—can barely imagine what it has taken to return Beach Haven, Long Beach Island, and, indeed, every hard-hit Jersey destination to this degree of orderly calm. No sand in *these* streets. So much shored up and shined.

We read about the millions upon millions of dollars. We hear of the waged wars with insurance carriers. We extend our gratitude for the pluck and perseverance. We empathize with those who have chosen not to return.

And, also: We know that it is a new age. We begin to agree—at last—on the lessons that must be learned about planetary fragility, the dangers ahead, last chances. We live in a time when we are being exhorted to "think like the Dutch," to weigh rebuilding strategies, to "promote resilience through innovative planning and design," to think, in a considered way, about barrier islands and why they exist and what might be done to protect them.

Spring is verging on summer now. The big wheel at Fantasy Island is poised to turn.

EARTHLY AMBITIONS

Bryn Mawr Farmers' Market

All week long I am thinking about ambition. The things we want and why we want them. The adjuration of enough.

I sit in the home of a poet and listen to him speak about choosing family over notoriety, quiet meals over the blustery pursuit of being widely known. I count the consequences of yearning for more—more opportunity, more visibility, more success, whatever success actually is. I think about how much more honest and unthwarted friendship means than a you-are-the-winner life.

Blustery pursuits. More and more. It can be dangerous stuff.

I'm still pondering Saturday morning, when I set out for the Bryn Mawr Farmers' Market, one of a number of Farm to City marketplaces that celebrate local farmers and food artisans. (Farm to City markets can also be found in Rittenhouse Square, University Square, on East Passyunk, Girard, and Moyamensing, and in Havertown, Chestnut Hill, and Swarthmore.) The temperature is a rare seventy degrees. The skies are blue. The air is breeze. The white tents in Bryn Mawr's Municipal Lot 7 have about them a carnival mood.

I cross the street. I'm in.

At the Herbal Springs Farmstead stand, two fifteen-year-old cousins, Alta and Brittany, are selling the strawberry, blueberry, and whoopee pies, the cinnamon buns and cookies they baked earlier in the week, pie after pie after pie. It is a substantial spread. It is a busy stand. I wonder out loud about the size of a kitchen that could produce such a feast. The girls look at each other and shrug. "The kitchen's not big," they say. "It's just big enough."

At the next stand, where John and Kira's chocolates are sold, the tag line is simple—*real people, REALLY good chocolates*—and the idea is hardly self-aggrandizing. Handmade chocolates in expertly built and labeled boxes. Natural ingredients drawn from family farms and urban gardens. Chocolates shaped like mushrooms, bees, and ladybugs. The size of John and Kira's dream.

At the Davidson Exotics Mushrooms stand, maitake, shitake, oyster, and portabellas—all picked just days before from Kennett Square earth—look exotic, even sexy, in their utilitarian boxes. At the Green Zebra Farm stand the talk is of tomato gravy, rainbow chard, four-pepper ketchup, and the pleasures of eating well. At the Brûlée Bakery stand, everything sweet is also gluten free, and at the Blue Elephant Garden stand, jars of happy-go-lucky summery meadowflower raw honey sit beside jars of something the company calls "sandwich rescue," which seeks (the height of its ambition) to outdo mayonnaise.

Kohlrabi, garlic scapes, radishes, turnips, still a little dirt on them. Homemade soup, homemade hummus, homemade hard cider, homemade gelato, homemade guacamole, natural beef, fresh eggs, bread, homegrown flowers. At one end of the market, at Tandi's Naturals, a woman named Gretchen is selling glycerin-rich handmade soaps, and at the other a pair of rescued garden shears is being sharpened back to life. In between, the signs or the talk points to Ephrata, Downingtown, Newtown Square, Northeast Philly, Chester Springs, Lancaster City, East Earl, and Havertown, and while there is but a single thoroughfare and it is the middle of the morning, the market bustles. I walk up and down. I taste and listen.

There is the rising sophomore at Dickinson College who is grateful for her parents' lessons in healthy eating. "I feel so much better when I am eating whole foods," she says.

There is the former fashion designer with the exquisite tattoos who sells the happy honey—while back home in Mount Airy, her own urban garden grows and awaits new chickens. "Nature," she says, tilting her face to the sun. "Why would you turn to anything else?"

There is the slender woman with a master's degree in public policy who yesterday handpicked the strawberries in the box right there and who can tell you, if you ask, about the faces on each juicy fruit. She's saving to buy a farm of her own, she confesses. She's studying strawberries and chard for their lessons.

There are the customers who always come back because it's the right thing to do. There are the people who are saying—as they taste the cheese, order the soup, buy a basket of bright flowers, put ice into the bag of their freshly bought lamb, ask for a second container of guac—what a privilege it is to support a Saturday-morning enterprise in which the food (and that glycerin-rich soap) comes from a cared-for place.

What we want, and why we want it. If there is a right *enough,* I've found it.

"What does it take," I ask the proprietor of Birchrun Hills, who has been explaining Equinox, Fat Cat, and Blue to a tempted customer, "to make an exceptional cheese?" He doesn't even blink. "Love," he says. "You can taste it in the cows' milk. You can taste it in the cheese."

NOTES ON HER MEMORY

Washington Memorial Chapel
at Valley Forge National Historical Park

We buried my mother on a January day—into the slope of a hill, under the naked arms of trees, beneath broken earth and petals. Everything depended on where you stood. There was sun, and there was shadow. There was warmth, and there was chill. I had felt my mother's spirit lift on the night she died. I felt it hover, still.

Later my father and I would design a red-granite headstone—birds taking flight, lambs seeking rest, a tree in full flower. Later my father would build her a garden—daffodils, phlox, begonia—and on the scorched days (and with permission) connect a long hose to a distant spigot to keep the blooms alive. Later we would bring wreaths (winter) and gifts (spring)—a miniature ornament, the cut sleeves of an oak-leaf hydrangea, words from my son, stories.

It is your birthday.
It is Christmas Eve.
We miss you.

The deer looked on. Warblers. Red-winged blackbirds. Fox.

Beyond my mother's stone, the thirty-five hundred acres of the Valley Forge National Historical Park rolled past. The Knox Estate greenhouse with its teeth of broken glass. The covered bridge, cool as the interior of a shell. The National Memorial Arch (a public discourse) and the redoubts (private knolls) and the spoked and grounded limbs of the Pawling sycamore and Washington's temporary home. In the months just after my mother's death, I was particularly obsessed with the greenhouse. Rust where seeds might have been. Gears that could not turn. Sunlight caught in a cage.

When your mother is buried at Valley Forge National Historical Park, you look to monumental land for signs of the eternal. I studied the trenchant greenhouse for a long time before I finally sought solace in the park's carillon—in the songs that have floated down from the National Patriots Bell Tower of the Washington Memorial Chapel for many decades now.

They are born of bronze, these songs—of fifty-eight separate, stationary bells that collectively weigh twenty-six tons. The oak keys that lever the bells are called batons and the invisible magistrate of music is called the carillonneur, and there are, I have read, twenty-four pedals at his feet—twenty-four ways to burnish sound.

The carillonneur burnishes sound.

These days, years after the passing of my mother, I will park my car by the chapel and walk down past the used-book store and the Cabin Shop and the well-fed cats until I'm standing in the burial grounds. The churchyard slopes. It is bisected by thin roads (lots named for Generals Poor and Rochambeau, Scott and Varnum and Wayne) and fringed by trees (sentinels with leafy hats). The individual plots are marked by polished and unpolished stones, by names and years, by erupted tree roots and weathered mementos, by abbreviated elegies: Beloved. Father. Friend.

From up above, where the carillonneur sits in the tall stone tower, it might all resemble a well-embroidered quilt. I myself, if viewed from above, might resemble whom I've finally become—the grown daughter of a missing mother and of a father who daily sees a garden through.

A daughter, grown.

By the time I've reached my mother's grave, the carillon songs will have often begun. Hymns like lullabies. The soft, sweet crush of musical vowels. A Christmas carol or an anthem I can't name but have heard before—perhaps in childhood, perhaps in a foreign land. Up in his tower, the carillonneur will strike the batons with the backs of his fists and temper the notes with his feet, and down below, in the churchyard, I will momentarily believe that the song is for me. That is not true. The bronzed bells play for my mother and also for the child buried nearby and for the father and sister and soldiers and sons who lie beneath the quilted land. They play for the deer and the fox, the warblers and red-winged blackbirds, and they are cloud cover, and their notes fall like rain. The carillonneur's songs are unbidden and given. They are binding and free. They, like the seasons, like life itself, go on.

I'll stand by my mother's grave, listening. I'll stand telling her the stories of the world as it has clocked forward—the new news, the old concerns, the tremor of recurring myths. I'll stand admiring my father's handiwork—which is not just the way his flowers grow but the way he proves steadfast. Sometimes the carillonneur will have stopped playing before I'm gone, but the echoes remain—in the trees, in the grass, in the blooms. They will have seeped their way into a daughter's thoughts and into a red-granite garden.

THE LIGHTS FANTASTIC

Montgomery and Delaware Counties,
Tredyffrin and Willistown Townships

In late December, we went searching for light.

After the stories had been told, the recorder played, the piano attempted ("O Holy Night"). After the fried sardines of the Eve and the feast of the Day (a turkey too big for its pan, desserts stashed beneath dishtowels in the narrow sewing room). After our uncle, ever mischievous, subverted the games our mother thought we might play. After the opening of the gifts that had been bought so far in advance that our parents mostly couldn't remember what the bowed-up boxes contained.

Into the car we would climb. If there had been snow, we would listen for its crunch beneath the wheels and watch the world through the long yellow eyes of the headlights. The crystal hats on the houses. The icicle beards on the mailboxes. The snowmen with their stick arms and their stiffened scarves. The sleeves of freeze on bent-necked trees. The channels and ruts where the sleds had made their way down modest hills.

Even if the snow had not yet arrived or had already (cruelly) vanished, we found what we were looking for, because it was always there, it always is—the lights of Christmas. Persistent blue bulbs and glamorized pines. Crèche scenes and delineating haloes. Pellucid angel wings and peppy Santas. Rudolphs dazzled by their own red snouts and candles on sills and the secrets of interior trees and the feverish electric blink of Yuletide excess—like Atlantic City, we thought, like an airport runway.

It was variations on awe.

It was hush.

It was suburban Wilmington when we were young and suburban Philadelphia when we got older. It was always my father behind the wheel, because he was the one with the innate talent for hunting down the lights fantastic. We never asked him where he was going; he just drove—away from the house on Maple Shade, down the back roads of Haverford, along the outer hem of Broomall, into the dark swerves of Newtown Square. Small roads paralleling big roads. The friendly loops of cul-de-sacs. The notched ups and downs and arounds of Darby-Paoli Road, where it was dark except when it glowed and where the daytime herd of cows never did make a starlit appearance.

Where had they gone?

We drove—or, rather, our father did. We hardly spoke, save for the short verbs (*Look*), the exclamations (*Wow*), the necessary adjectives. It was like going to the movies in reverse—we moved, the scenes stayed still. It was like going window shopping, but there was nothing to buy. It was like getting away with something, but hunting for light is never a crime.

Finally, of course, we'd turn back toward the house where our holidays had begun—the house with the half-eaten turkey still in the pan and the gifts unwrapped and the games subverted. In our slow and usually silent approach along the bend of the last road, we could see, for an instant, our own lives lit as mysteriously and spectacularly as the strangers whose homes we'd just spied on. The shimmer of that big tree through the window. The white wings of the angels in the yard. The illuminating lights beneath the twin wreaths.

Who was lucky enough to live there? We were lucky enough to live there. It caught us, fabulously, by surprise.

Now, when the days grow short and the air is brittle, I find myself behind the wheel, on the hunt for lights—sometimes alone, sometimes with company. I'll head back to the wide back streets of Wayne, where the interiors are amber and mistletoed and the outsides are bright. I'll drive down Goshen Road to Willistown—past the horse farms and the preserves and Bartram's Covered Bridge. I'll steer toward Lancaster Avenue and its parade of lit-up snowflakes. I'll drive the streets where I live.

I'll stop at lanterns.

I'll consider rooflines.

I'll watch a dozen Santas blink.

I'll want nothing that I can buy.

And sometimes I'll stop by the side of a road named Church, where there is little, in one glorious stretch, but a long wooden fence and winter grass and sky itself, on the horizon. I'll turn the key and climb out of the car and watch the last versions of the sun fall down while the first versions of the stars rise up—scintillated spacklings of bright.

I'll count the colors that blink on and off.

Another variation on awe.

HOME

This old house on this leafy street is quantifiable—a museum of animating things. A gesso wing. A palm-sized table. An envelope of watercolors. A few frames of funny men who wear their eyeballs on their sleeves. Bisqued faces, glazed vessels, pots in ancient earth tones. Like sun on water, like pink in clouds, like an egg in the nest of the tree, they hang, they sit, they wait, they tremble.

They are.

The books slouch triple thick on shelves or tall in corner stacks or quiet and aware in dark, underneath places. The photographs are the ones we took, or that others took—Salvadoran landscapes, a cratered lake, Venice in winter, Florence in autumn, Spoleto in the heat, Seville in the earliest parts of day, a gorgeous dark-haired son who grows up (*There he is*) frame by frame.

There are glass apples on the windowsill, and a girl built of sticks with a bird on her head, and a sleek wooden giraffe that stands by the window looking out, and also two fine spinning wheels, a cluster of dried lotus pods, a closet full of faded baseball caps, a high school jacket on a hanger.

There is a hummingbird's nest in a plastic bag and the tip of a tail of a baby lamb and a pair of glass fox eyes and the skull of a pine marten, and (in an adjacent place) a self-portrait built of crayon wax. In the kitchen: jars of powdered chocolate and spices, a bag of saffron, recipes for the cookies he liked best until my father gave me my mother's recipe book and I learned how to make her brownies. In the window: papier-mâché girls in flowered dresses hanging from transparent strings. Girls in flowered dresses beneath the shelter of balloons and kites.

In the bowl: a ripening pear.

Outside the wind chimes cling to a gnarly place in the trumpet vine, and the garden is an archipelago that blooms and suffers, and along the back of the house the bulbs of daffodils and gladioli do their inevitable things, and there is a soccer goal net that hasn't been used for years, beneath the awning of trees.

This is the house.

This is what remains when the child who grew up frame by frame moves on—still dark-haired, now tall. "Love you," his text comes in. Or, "Just saw Mike Tyson get out of a car." Or, "Taking a walk by the river. Beautiful." Or, "Figured out the start of my next story." Or, "Work is good. Got a new account." Flash nonfictions. News from the other side. Reports from the son who has a brilliant life of his own, in a city of his own, in a room of his own.

His own house.

His own things.

"You won't believe what I just heard," he texts.

"I think it's going to snow," he texts.

"Just saw Jason Stratham while eating dinner."

Our children move on, their lives accelerate, their worlds are as big and as glorious as they make them, and that, of course, is what we want best and most, what gives us peace. Throughout it all, the old house stays where it was on the leafy street with the rather random garden and the leftover goal and the excess of baseball caps and the perfect crayon portrait.

The light changes. The quality of silence. There are shifts in the meaning of things. Background migrates toward foreground. Time takes on a gentle ping.

So that we sit for a longer time with the book of snapshots on our laps. *He was so small, we were so young, we danced like that.* So that we stand beside the giraffe, looking out on the street—two sentinels watching and remembering. So that we suddenly recall why we bought the glass eyes in the first place and why we could not leave Asheville without that girl with the bird on her head and why it was that we came to collect the nearly weightless girls that hang from their transparent strings, in their many flowered dresses.

In the absence of the children that we will always fiercely love, we have these things, these vessels, these funny faces, these eyes on sleeves, these ancient tomes and buckling photographs, these places where our memories live. We have what we made, what we bought, what we read, what we saved, what we could offer, what we knew how to be, where we walked, and the stories we brought home.

We have what we became.

It's all here, nearer, somehow, than it used to be.

CREDITS AND ACKNOWLEDGMENTS

The following essays first appeared, in slightly different form, and in some cases with different titles, in the *Philadelphia Inquirer:*

"Preface"
"Treasure Hunt"
"Time In, Time Out"
"The Ghosts of Bush Hill"
"Them, Then; Us, Now"
"Into the Woods"
"River Redemption"
"*psychylustro*"
"City Sidewalks"
"Room for a View"
"The Students Stay Young; the Teacher Grows Old"
"Body Language"
"So Many Doors, So Many Windows"
"Of Feathers and Fur"
"The Artist and the Foundrymen"
"All in the House"
"Things Are Disappearing Here"
"Essential Dualities"
"Past, Present, Future"
"Double Dipping"

"Garden Retreat in the High Heat of Summer"
"Heart on the Horses"
"I Thought I Could Dance"
"Accidental Tourists"
"After the Storm"
"Earthly Ambitions"
"Notes on Her Memory"
"The Lights Fantastic"

The essay "Home" first appeared, in slightly different form, on the *Psychology Today* blog, edited by Jennifer Haupt.

The essay "On a Wing and a Prayer" first appeared, in different form, in *Weekend* magazine.

The essay "Skytop Lodge" first appeared in *Philadelphia Magazine.*

I have written about Bruce Springsteen previously—on my blog and in *Poets' Quarterly.* I can't seem to help myself.

All photographs by and © Beth Kephart.

My thanks:

To Avery Rome, *Philadelphia Inquirer* projects editor. You invited me to think out loud about our city and our private spheres. I will always be grateful for the door you opened and for your exquisite wisdom.

To Kevin Ferris, assistant editor of the *Philadelphia Inquirer* board. We met for tea and we never looked back. Our collaboration and our friendship remain a bright light in my life. For all the advice and generosity through these many declarations and expositions, I thank you.

To Jackie Rose, for facilitating the *Philadelphia Inquirer* permissions process.

To those who have dreamed, believed, restored, advocated, and become my friends: Karen Young and Ellen Shultz of Fairmount Water Works; Joe Syrnick of Schuylkill Banks; Kurt Zwikl and Laura Catalano of Schuylkill River Heritage Area; Jerry Sweeney of Brandywine Realty Trust; Bill Thomas of Chanticleer Garden; Barbara Bassett of Philadelphia Art Museum; Andrew Kahan of Free Library of Philadelphia; Jane Golden of Philadelphia Mural Arts Program; Greg Djanikian of University of Pennsylvania; Matt Cabrey of Select Greater Philadelphia; Elizabeth Dow of Leadership Philadelphia; John Rollins of Friends of Wissahickon, Julie Diana and Zak Hench, formerly of Pennsylvania Ballet; and my many friends at both DanceSport Academy and Wayne Art Center.

To the Temple team—Micah Kleit, my editor, who once again kindly said yes; to Ann-Marie Anderson, who picks up the phone when I call—and listens; to Gary Kramer, who magnificently sends out word; to Sara Jo Cohen, who has all the answers; to Joan Vidal, who keeps us on track; to Kate Nichols, for the cover and the interior; to Debby Smith, my copy editor, for her patience; and to Mary Rose Muccie, at the helm.

To Amy Rennert, who has been here since day one.

To my father, who gave me the kind of unwavering support that enables a child, a student, a woman to see. To my husband, who stands by as I love out loud. To my son, who understands, perhaps better than anyone, my passion for the place I live and, to this day, walks far and wide with me.

Beth Kephart is the award-winning author of twenty books, including *Going Over, Handling the Truth: On the Writing of Memoir, Flow: The Life and Times of Philadelphia's Schuylkill River,* and *Ghosts in the Garden: Reflections on Endings, Beginnings, and the Unearthing of Self.* She has been nominated for a National Book Award, has been awarded grants from the National Endowment for the Arts and the Pew Fellowships in the Arts, and has won the national Speakeasy Poetry Prize. Kephart writes a monthly column on the intersection of memory and place for the *Philadelphia Inquirer* and is a frequent contributor to the *Chicago Tribune.* She teaches memoir at the University of Pennsylvania and blogs daily at www.beth-kephart.blogspot.com.